The Family
and the State
Considerations for social policy

To Peggy

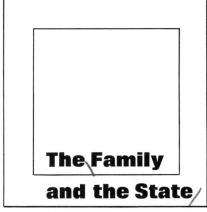

The Family
and the State
Considerations for social policy

Robert M. Moroney

Longman
London and New York

Longman Group Limited London

Associated companies, branches and representatives throughout the world

Published in the United States of America by Longman Inc., New York

© Longman Group Limited, 1976

First published 1976

Library of Congress Cataloging in Publication Data

Moroney, Robert,
    The family and the state.

    Includes index.
    1. Family—Great Britain.   2. Public welfare—Great Britain.
    3. Great Britain—Social policy.   4. Family social work—Great Britain.
    5. Community health services—Great Britain.   6. Handicapped—Family
    relationships.   I. Title.
HQ622.M67   362.8'2'0941   75—45230
ISBN 0 582 48493 6 paper

Set in IBM Theme 10 on 11pt
and printed in Great Britain by
Lowe and Brydone (Printers) Ltd,
Thetford, Norfolk

Contents

List of tables   vi

Preface *Robin Huws Jones, Joseph Rowntree Memorial Trust*   ix

Acknowledgements   xi

1 The family and social policy   1

A social policy approach — Ambiguities in social welfare policy — Current views on the family: fact or myth? — The family and the State: the nature of the relationship — Plan of the study

2 The family and the caring function   15

Functions of the family — Characteristics of the modern family — Implications of these changes for families — Families and the provision of social care — Summary

3 The family and the elderly   34

Characteristics of the elderly — Functional status of the elderly — Living status of the elderly — Community-based care — Discussion

4 The family and the mentally handicapped child   63

Historical background and definitional problems — The prevalence of mental handicap — Characteristics of the severely mentally handicapped — Effects of mental handicap on the family — Institutional trends — Community services — Discussion

5 The family and the State: qualitative and quantitative aspects of a caring function   92

Dimensions of a caring society: choice, support and shared responsibility — The issue of resource constraints — Organizational barriers to the provision of services — Manpower: the critical role of the social worker — Summary

6 The family, the State and social policy   116

Shared responsibility — Family responsibility in a Welfare State — The issue of family policy — Summary and conclusions

Index   141

Abbreviations used in references

CSO   *Central Office of Statistics*
DHSS *Department of Health and Social Security*
GSS   *Government Statistical Service*
OPCS *Office of Population Censuses and Surveys*

List of tables

2.1   Family size 1860—1970, England and Wales   18

2.2   Female participation rate in the work force, 1921—91, England and Wales   19

2.3   Dependency ratio, 1851—1971, England and Wales   20

2.4   Per cent married women aged 45—60 in the work force, 1921—71, England and Wales   21

2.5   Caretaker pool, 1901—71, United Kingdom   22

2.6   Permanent housing completed, 1945—73, England and Wales   23

3.1   Per cent increase in the elderly population, 1901—2001, England and Wales   35

3.2   Social welfare expenditure on the elderly   35

3.3   Elderly population as percentage of total population, England and Wales   36

3.4   Age and sex distribution of the elderly population, 1951—2001, England and Wales   37

3.5   Marital status of the elderly, 1901—2001, England and Wales   38

3.6   Prevalence of incapacity, impairment and limitations among the elderly: three surveys   40

3.7   Number of very severely handicapped elderly, 1971—2001, England and Wales   41

3.8   Residential status of elderly, 1911—71, England and Wales   42

3.9   Living status of non-institutional elderly, 1971, Great Britain   43

3.10   Percentage of elderly who received help from families   44

3.11   Living status of non-institutionalized elderly handicapped, England and Wales   44

3.12   Trends in residential care, 1906—73, England and Wales   47

3.13   Trends in long-term residential care, 1911—73, England and Wales   48

3.14   Residential care rates per 1,000 elderly, 1958—59 and 1971, England and Wales   49

3.15   Projections of institutional elderly population, England and Wales   50

3.16 Utilization trends — selected community services, rates per 1,000 elderly, 1958—73, England and Wales 52

3.17 Per cent increase in utilization of selected community services and whole-time equivalent manpower, 1967—71, England and Wales 55

3.18 Utilization of community services by the handicapped elderly, 1968, Great Britain 56

3.19 Trends in social welfare expenditure for selected services — percentages by service, 1958—71, England and Wales 57

4.1 Estimated prevalence of severe mental handicap, 1951—2001, England and Wales 68

4.2 Incapacity associated with severe mental handicap 69

4.3 Mentally handicapped patients in hospital care, 1952—71, England and Wales 72

4.4 Admissions to institutions for the mentally handicapped, 1952—71, England and Wales 73

4.5 Admission rates per 100,000 population to institutions for the mentally handicapped, 1949—66 74

4.6 Admissions and discharges, institutions for the mentally handicapped, 1964—66 75

4.7 Discharges from institutions for the mentally handicapped by length of stay, 1964—66 75

4.8 Estimates of the percentage of severely mentally handicapped in institutions, 1952—70, England and Wales 76

4.9 Distribution of the institutional population by age and degree of handicap, 1970, England and Wales 77

4.10 Institutional and non-institutional severely mentally handicapped by age and incapacity 78

4.11 Number of mentally handicapped known to local authorities, 1947—70, England and Wales 79

4.12 Number of severely mentally handicapped under local authority care, 1963—70, England and Wales 80

4.13 Number of severely mentally handicapped in residential care, 1963—70, England and Wales 81

4.14 Number of severely mentally handicapped in training centres, 1963—70, England and Wales 82

4.15 Number of severely mentally handicapped boarding out or in private homes at local authority expense, 1963—70, England and Wales 83

4.16   Utilization rates of various community services by the severely mentally handicapped, 1970   86

5.1   Public expenditure and expenditures on social welfare as percentage of the gross national product, 1900–73   98

5.2   *Per capita* expenditure on social welfare, United Kingdom   99

6.1   Constant attendance allowances: utilization rate and prevalence of handicapping conditions, 1973, England and Wales   133

Preface

Is the family today less willing or less able to care for its severely dependent members, for instance frail old people or mentally handicapped children? Apparently, many responsible and informed people in Britain and in other countries believe that it is less able, less willing, or both, and a recent Report of the U.K. Central Policy Review Staff urges the need to consider the consequences of the possibly declining capacity and willingness of families to care for their own social casualties. But firm evidence is hard to come by; even the terms used are debatable, the data is sketchy and the analysis proves highly complex; in the end it is easy to reach opposite conclusions.

It would be surprising if the patterns of family care had not changed over the last two generations. The proportion of married women who go out to work has risen dramatically; the traditional 'caretaker', the unmarried daughter or aunt, is a disappearing phenomenon; the nature of dependancy (though not the overall proportion) has changed, with fewer children and more old people; the increased survival of severely handicapped children and very old people has altered the dimensions of family care. Social policies, it is claimed, have in some ways made family care more difficult, for instance new housing estates have by their distance unintentionally weakened the informal support of aged parents by their families.

As the institutions that provide for severely dependent people improve, families must wonder whether they are doing best for their very dependent members by keeping them at home, when they might have more expert treatment and a higher standard of living in some hospitals or hostels. Indeed, there is evidence that care at home, however devoted and willing, is not always in the best interest of the handicapped person, or the other members of the family, especially other children.

The issue is not merely academic; if even a small proportion of the families now providing for their severely handicapped members were to press the statutory services to take over, the results could be calamitous, at least in the short run. As this enquiry shows, this is by no means unthinkable; in Denmark for instance the rates of residential care for the elderly are almost twice as high as in the U.K, and the current institutional care of mentally handicapped people is 20 per cent higher than the *target* proposed by the Department of Health and Social Services.

It was with questions like these in mind that the Joseph Rowntree Memorial Trust decided that it would be useful to promote a survey of the changing patterns of family care, bringing together the available data, seeking the views of people who work closely with these problems, analysing trends, and considering their social implications.

It was decided to commission an independent study, that might be described as a social scientist's equivalent of the geologist's surface survey. The subject could absorb a life time but in this preliminary study, it was decided to aim at a report to be completed within twelve months.

Dr Robert Moroney of the Department of City and Regional Planning at the University of North Carolina bravely agreed to undertake this task. He has brought together much important material and has attempted, as far as we know for the first time, a focussed and systematic analysis of the changing relationship between the state and the family in modern Britain in relation to the care of severely dependent people. He has contributed significantly to the methodology of social policy analysis.

The Trust is indebted to him for his industry and skill, for his obvious concern with the core questions, and for the way in which he has set out his findings.

Dr Moroney would be the last to suggest that he has found final answers. In the nature of the task, it is inevitable that some readers, differing in their background or their values, will challenge some of the data and dispute some of the interpretations and conclusions. But Dr Moroney has set out important hypotheses which must command attention; he has pointed to current trends that policy makers and social administrators will ignore at their peril, and especially at other people's peril. For instance, the current emphasis on 'priorities' in the personal social services must mean that services will increasingly be diverted to those who need total care (with the state as a substitute family) rather than to families who look after their own handicapped members (the state as partner in supporting the family).

In his conclusions one central finding emerges: on balance, the evidence does not support the view that the modern family is giving up its caring function, or transferring its traditional responsibilities to the state.

Dr Moroney indicates areas where further work is urgently required. His study, is likely to prove a quarry that will be mined for a long time.

The Joseph Rowntree Memorial Trust thanks Dr Moroney for his valuable work, and his University for giving him leave of absence. The Trust also wishes to express its appreciation of all those, particularly the members of the Advisory Committee, Professor Robert Morris of Brandeis University and Dr Alvin Schorr of the New York Community Service Society who generously gave their time to help this exploration.

R. Huws Jones

Acknowledgements

In his preface to the *Gift Relationship*, Titmuss stated that in writing that book he had 'incurred many social debts . . . gifts solicited and unsolicited, in the form of advice and criticism'. This book is also the product of many individuals' interest and support and it is impossible fully to acknowledge their contributions.

Although he died the year before I reached England, Titmuss had a major role in shaping the study. Like so many other Americans involved in the field of social policy/social administration, I have admired his ability to clarify issues, to raise discomforting but critical questions, and his talent in presenting complex data in a fresh and often exciting way. It is one thing to be competent in a technical sense, it is another to capture the interest of such diverse groups of people as political figures, civil servants, academics, students, social welfare practitioners and the general public. Few people have these 'gifts' but all of us have a role model.

I find myself in debt to three others who have also had a significant impact on the formation of social policy. One is Robin Huws Jones, formerly with the National Institute for Social Work Training and now with the Joseph Rowntree Memorial Trust. His contribution to this study was multifaceted. He not only was a guiding force for the study; he also gave support, a critical sounding board, introductions to key administrators and practitioners, and thorough readings of various drafts of the manuscript. Two Americans, Robert Morris of the Florence Heller School for Advanced Studies in Social Welfare, Brandeis University and Alvin Schorr, General Director of the Community Service Society, New York, deserve special acknowledgement. Both are noted for their ability to blend a sense of reality with a vision of what is possible in the future. Each willingly gave time in the early phases of this study, particularly in suggesting strategies for dealing with such a complex issue as family care and family supports.

The study was financed by the Joseph Rowntree Memorial Trust, a remarkable institution in that it is interested in supporting the exploration of an issue that may have significant consequences for the future. The Trust, through Lewis Waddilove and Robin Huws Jones also assembled an advisory group for the project that included, in addition to themselves, Joan Cooper, Director of Social Work Services, DHSS; Walter Holland, Department of Clinical Epidemiology and Social Medicine, St Thomas's Hospital Medical School; A. R. Isserlis, Director, Centre for Studies in Social Policy; N. Jordan Moss, Deputy Secretary, DHSS; Jack Tizard, Institute of Education, University of London. At various stages, they offered invaluable insights and later reviewed drafts of the manuscripts.

While I benefited from discussions with literally scores of practitioners and administrators from the public and voluntary sectors, I would like to single out for special comment: Mrs M. Parfitt, Director of Social Services, Dyfed; D. T. White, Director of Social Services, Coventry; P. Westland, Director of Social Services, Hammersmith; P. Hughes, Director of Social Services, Wakefield. Their interest in and contribution to the study was considerable.

Finally, I would like to thank A. R. Isserlis, the Fellows and staff of the Centre for Studies in Social Policy for a personally satisfying and professionally rewarding year. Their warmth and willingness to involve a visiting Fellow in the overall activities of the Centre and their patience in orienting a foreigner to the 'British scene' was an unanticipated benefit. Special thanks to Claudine McCready, J. Barnes and J. Lewis for finding the time to review and comment on the manuscript. Barbara Hughes from the Centre staff took on the onerous responsibility for the preparation of the manuscript through its numerous phases. I cannot thank her enough.

A final note is in order. While some of the comments made in this book may appear to be critical of social policies and social services in the United Kingdom, such is not intended. I personally am a great admirer of this system and compared to other countries, particularly my own, British social welfare is far advanced.

We are grateful to the following for permission to reproduce copyright material:

George Allen and Unwin Ltd for a table from *Plans & Provisions For The Mentally Handicapped* by Bone, Spain and Martin; Cambridge University Press for a table from *Demography* by P. Cox, published by Cambridge University Press; The Controller of Her Majesty's Stationery Office for tables and selected data from various Government Publications; Macmillan Publishers Ltd and St Martin's Press, Inc. for a table from *Trends in British Society* by A. H. Halsey, 1972, reprinted by permission of Macmillan London and Basingstoke and St Martin's Press Inc.; National Bureau of Economic Research Inc. for tables from *The Growth of Public Expenditure in the United Kingdom* by Alan T. Peacock and Jack Wiseman, 1961; Prentice-Hall Inc. for a table from *Social Structure and the Family: General Relations* by Shanas and Streib, reprinted by permission of Prentice-Hall Inc., Englewood Cliffs, New Jersey; Routledge and Kegan Paul Ltd and Aldine Publishing Company for a table from *Old People in Three Industrial Societies* by E. Shanus *et al.*

1 The family and social policy

This study is concerned with families, the function of the family as a social service (in the sense that it provides social care for its members) and conversely, the role of the organized welfare system as it affects the family. The underlying thesis is that while professionals and lay people hold many views related to this issue, its facets and long-term implications for social policy requirements have been neglected.

Recognition that the overwhelming majority of the handicapped are in the community and are being cared for by their families with varying degrees of support from public and voluntary agencies has only recently begun to emerge. The family has been instrumental in preventing or delaying the long-term admission to institutions of persons who are severely physically and mentally handicapped thus reducing a potentially heavy demand on social welfare services. Many families, often with the help of friends and neighbours, have provided what can only be described as a staggering amount of care. Other families have, for any number of reasons, sought long-term institutional care for family members. Many others may have mixed feelings. Whatever the outcome, the family is one of the few social institutions that appears to have existed throughout recorded history in one form or another and has carried the caring function of its dependent members. In this sense it has been a resource for family members and it is becoming increasingly clear that it has been a significant resource for the social welfare system.

There are some indications that many of these families, in providing support, are undergoing considerable stress and it is conceivable that some are beginning to question the desirability of current policy emphasis, whether implicit or explicit, on community care. The idea of community care itself may be partially the cause. It cannot be equated with family care, but rather has come to mean the provision of care to certain groups of dependent people in the community rather than in the large institutions of the Poor Law era. One problem has continued to be the lack of adequate community care services, while another appears to be some ambivalence as to its purposes. Both need to be evaluated in terms of how they affect families who have been and may want to continue providing the major caring function. Other factors may be related to changes in the institutions themselves. For example, as care in hospitals and various residential settings has improved; as the image of Poor Law institutions for the elderly, the mentally ill and mentally handicapped fades, more and more responsible families may begin to wonder whether their decision to provide care in the home is in the best interest of the handicapped member in terms of their physical and social wellbeing. Not only are there perceived benefits for the handicapped member, but given the nature and intensity of the strain on the total family unit, families may feel that alternatives to family care are more desirable for the wellbeing of others living in the home. This scenario in no way is meant to imply that the issue can be viewed as either institutional care or family care. These are only two among many alternatives, alternatives that may reflect some combination of both.

If there is a growing trend in this direction, if families are expecting society in general and the State in particular to assume increased responsibilities for the handicapped, and if this trend were to be expressed in greater demands on the social welfare services, this would have important social and economic ramifications. In policy terms, this concern might be posed by two types of questions. What would happen if even 5 or 10 per cent of the families who now look after their handicapped members were to ask the public sector to assume this function? The country is faced with immense economic problems that are likely to continue for a number of years. The emphasis is now for cutbacks in public expenditure, and pressure is being placed on local authorities to limit their activities to those considered necessary. The issue is not determining priorities for expansion in the social welfare services, but one of controlled retrenchment. Compounding this is the general recognition that severe shortages in specific services exist already. The State, therefore, has taken the position that it cannot meet existing need let alone additional responsibilities. This aspect is dealt with in Chapter 5.

The second policy question is more basic to the issue of public expenditure. If there is a shift in transfer from the family to the State, is it in fact the unintended consequence of existing social policies? Are families actually being influenced in this direction, are they doing so because the family as a social institution is changing, or is it the result of some interaction between both phenomena?

A social policy approach

While the issue raised is fairly clear in general terms, the selection of a strategy to shed light on it is much more complex. There is, by and large, no universal agreement as to what social policy is, its boundaries, nor appropriate methodologies for its analysis[1]*. The approach to the specific issue of this study was shaped by a belief that social policy is concerned with a search for and articulation of social objectives and the means to achieve these. While this presupposes a normative position expressing some sense of predetermined values, it is built upon a number of non-ideological activities. Policy formulation and development requires analysis of the issue, its dimensions and its implications. It further necessitates a consensus of the body politic that the situation presents a current or future problem that should be addressed. Finally it involves decision-making, choosing among alternative strategies and developing structures to carry out specific interventions.

This study covers the first phase of this process, the clarification of the

*References appear at the end of each chapter.

issue through the presentation of relevant data; the identification, where possible, of factors associated with the issue; and the tracing through of implications of any discernible trends. Although it is recognized that the actual shaping of the questions to be studied may reflect a personal bias on the part of the person carrying out the study, this activity, the cornerstone of the policy process, is not prescription but description. The aim of the analysis is to raise a variety of questions from a range of sources and to some extent to provide the necessary corrective to the bias. The policy analysis phase clarifies and sharpens the discussion but it cannot, nor should it, dictate what is to be done. Ultimately in a democratic society decision-making is the responsibility of politicians who are held accountable by those they represent.

If the study were to identify an increasing transfer of responsibility for the care of the socially dependent from the family to the organized social welfare system, these trends and their social and economic implications need to be anticipated and factors associated with the shift should be identified. For example, if the increased transfer is found to be a part of a larger evolutionary process in which the nature of the family itself is changing, society might be expected to respond by changing its perception of the caring function. If on the other hand, families are merely responding to social policies that they interpret as encouragement or even pressure to give up this responsibility, the issue changes. The first conclusion would suggest that the shift arises from changing family behaviour and expectations, the latter would emphasize that the way in which society views its own function in the provision of care to the dependent is influencing these changes in the family. While it might prove impossible to identify a causal relationship, initially the issue should be posed in such a way that both possibilities are explored.

Evidence and its implications can then be used by those responsible for developing social policy. This is the second phase of the process, the labelling of the situation as a social problem and a statement of some desirable future state[2]. Unlike the first phase, this statement is normative and usually reflects both an ideological position and an appreciation of political constraints. Historically the key to the process is informal debate leading to some expression of consensus. It is here that the question changes to one that asks whether the family or society is assuming too much or too little responsibility for the caring function? Should there be specific policies to slow down or increase rates of institutionalization? Should policies be developed whose aim is to keep the socially dependent in their families at all costs? Should policies explicitly encourage the family to transfer the caring function to a greater degree? Should the purpose of the policies be primarily one of providing a series of meaningful alternatives to families so that they are able to make meaningful choices? What should be the appropriate relationship between the family and society, the family and the State? These are all questions of preference.

When sufficient consensus is reached for a policy decision to be made and a political preference has emerged, both short- and long-range strategies need to be developed. These are often shaped by the present state of technology and the availability of resources. Experts are often divided as to the best way to solve complex social problems, and choices have to be made between alternative strategies. The criteria of efficiency, effectiveness, coverage and eligibility are all part of this process of decision-making. Finally, administrative issues have to be resolved; for example, appropriate structures to carry out the policy, the manpower required, and whether the effort will be carried out by government, the voluntary sector, or some combination of both.

Thus social policy in this context is viewed as a blending of fact and preference that emerges from a continuous dialogue between the policy analyst, the policy maker, and the policy implementer. While the process is not necessarily orderly nor progressive, while roles can become merged and the boundaries between the phases fuzzy, these are the inputs[3].

Ambiguities in social welfare policy

The entire structure of the 'Welfare State' as it has evolved depends on a set of implicit and explicit assumptions concerning the responsibility which families assume, or are expected to assume, for their members and the conditions under which this responsibility must either be shared with or taken over by society through its public or voluntary organizations[4]. Historically, most social welfare programmes were developed on the premise that the family and the immediate neighbouring environment constituted the first line of responsibility when individuals had their self-maintaining capacities impaired or threatened. It was further expected that families would support these members until the situation became overwhelming and only then would society intervene[5].

This residual approach has gradually been replaced with the philosophy that society, especially as represented by its government, should assume more and more direct responsibility for assuring that the basic social and economic needs of its members be met. This evolution, at least in part, has been influenced by a growing awareness that many of the stresses facing families and individuals are beyond their control. They are the victims of broader social and economic forces rather than the cause of the problems. The Depression of the 1930s emphatically demonstrated that poverty and unemployment were not the result of individual failure and that solutions could not be found in the rehabilitation of the individual. This in turn led to an acceptance of the need for collective intervention in both economic and structural terms.

However, this forward movement has carried with it a number of uncertainties and the borderline between society assuming increased responsibility through its social welfare institutions and the family retaining appropriate functions has become less clear. In some areas there appears to be minimal disagreement, and this transfer of responsibility is generally accepted. In the United Kingdom as well as most Western societies the family is no longer viewed as responsible for the formal education of children nor the financial support of the aged. This is not meant to imply that there is a universal acceptance of the principle nor of the specific social welfare mechanisms that have been developed. There have been criticisms, but by and large they bear on ways to improve the institutions.

In many other areas, especially those outside the realm of financial support, the dividing line for this transfer, or in some cases the proportion to be shared by each, is seen as uneven and there appears to be an element of ambivalence as expressed in law, policy, programme and practice. Although society intervenes at increasing levels in a growing number of areas, the family is still expected to provide the basic support to its dependent members in a moral sense, whether they are children or aged, physically, emotionally or mentally handicapped. The principle of societal responsibility exists but how society and the State relate to the family is still ambiguous, and there have been few systematic studies of this issue. Troublesome questions are being raised more and more by political figures, administrators and academics. Many of these will be examined in this study, such as:

- Are there reasonable boundaries to this progressive shifting of responsibility from the family to society, in particular from the family to the public sector? How viable is the idea of shared responsibility?
- As new social policies are enacted and eventually translated into operational programmes, are they based on a realistic understanding of the presentday family, its ability and willingness (or conversely its inability or unwillingness) to participate in the care of the socially dependent, or do they assume a concept of the family that is either outmoded or never existed?
- Is it possible that by allocating greater amounts of social welfare resources, families and neighbours are inadvertently discouraged from continuing their participation in the caring function? Can increased supply create additional expectation and demand by adversely affecting the informal caring network that exists?
- Have there been shifts in expectation or behaviour on the part of families and professionals that have not been fully recognized but that have significant implications for future social policy?
- Has recent emphasis on the caring function created a correspondingly greater expectation of the family?

These questions are raised to highlight the fact that there are fundamental questions about which we know very little, fundamental in so far as they address the very essence of society. They are the concern of theologians and philosophers, sociologists and anthropologists, economists and political scientists, professionals and every member of a family. They are emotionally charged issues that evoke heated ideological debate. Thus they are vital social policy issues that require examination.

While a strong case could be made for a comprehensive mapping of the entire terrain of the relationship between the family and society as it relates to the care of the socially dependent, this particular study attempts to grapple with the issue on a more modest scale. Specifically, the focus covers families with physically and mentally handicapped members and attempts to explore the nature of the relationship between the family and the social welfare system. Narrowing the focus further the primary emphasis is placed on two distinct sub-groups of the handicapped: the frail elderly and the mentally handicapped child. The rationale for this is three-fold. First, the very nature of the pressures and problems these families face, the size of the 'at risk populations' and their requirements all have serious implications for future resource allocations. The second reason is more or less hypothetical. If there are any shifts in the relationship between the family and society in the care of the handicapped, it would probably be perceived initially with these two groups since both tend to be viewed by society at large as 'worthy' of support and their dependency is less stigmatized (in a relative sense). Neither the ageing process and more recently the occurrence of mental handicap is viewed as the fault of the individual nor of his family. For over thirty years, since the Beveridge Report the elderly have been identified in legislation as a group to be given high priority in the development of social programmes. Fifteen years later similar explicit policy statements emerged for the mentally handi-capped[6]. Words such as 'dignity' and 'rights' appear often and while a policy statement does not necessarily lead to full implementation of the policy, as an explicit posture it does shape attitudes. The final reason for limiting the study to two groups was simply one of time and manage-ability. However, even though the focus is limited, it was believed that the findings should have wider applicability to other groups of handicapped.

Current views on the family: fact or myth?

Although there is a lack of systematic analysis on this issue, this does not mean that it has been ignored. Current debate, especially in the political arena, argues that the family as an institution has changed over time, especially since the inception of the Welfare State and the postwar period. Not only has this institution changed in structure, form and activity patterns, but it is further charged that families today are less willing to carry out those functions that have historically been their responsibility. The strongest expression of this position is found in a recent address by a leading political figure:

They [the family and civilized values] are the foundation on which the nation is built; they are being undermined. If we cannot restore them to health, our nation can be utterly ruined, whatever economic policies we might try to follow.... The Socialist method would try to take away from the family and its members the responsibilities which give it cohesion. Parents are being divested of their duty to provide for their family economically, of their responsibility for education, health, up-

bringing, morality, advice and guidance, of saving for old age, for housing. When you take responsibility away from people, you make them irresponsible[7].

A statement such as this usually proves to be quite dysfunctional in so far as it evokes primarily emotional responses. One faction rushes to defend the conclusion as hard fact while another will reject it out of hand. The debate is concerned with values and deeply held beliefs. Those who believe that the Welfare State or socialism is responsible for the major problems facing the country will point to this as additional evidence to support their position, one more example. Others who defend socialism will counter with claims that the family is better off than in previous eras. This type of argument, based on values or ideology and using emotive labels such as deterioration and irresponsibility, all too easily drifts into an abstract debate about social ideals[8]. Battle-lines are quickly drawn and the challenges made. Each group knows what is good, what should be done. A more productive response, neither accepting nor rejecting the charge, would be to search for evidence that might clarify and sharpen the issue. Theoretically, two questions need to be raised. The first is concerned with the phenomenon. Has the family changed with regard to the caring function, and if so what are the facets of the change? The second question would follow if change is found. What are its implications and what are the factors associated with it? The need is not for additional emotional fuel to be thrown on this ideological fire, but for systematic analysis with change initially viewed as neither positive nor negative. Does it have a basis in fact?

These fears are not new. Sorokin raised the same warning as early as the 1920s when he spoke of the crisis facing Western society, a crisis that was destroying the fundamental form of society and culture. While he saw that this deterioration affected all social institutions his comments related to the family are most germane:

The Family is virtually non-existent nowadays, in contradistinction to the medieval family, or even that of a century ago. As it has become more and more contractual, the family of the last few decades has grown even more unstable, until it has reached the point of actual disintegration. . . .

. . . The result is rapidly mounting juvenile delinquency, an increasing number of young people without moral integrity, strength of character, a sense of social duty or spontaneous altruism, who swell the ranks of criminals, or irresponsible persons[9].

Thus we have the same observations made fifty years apart. The major difference is, of course, the identification of the causes of the 'deterioration, disintegration and irresponsibility' of the family. The more recent view cites socialism and the emergence of a particular form of the Welfare State. In extending its role, in assuming more functions, the State interferes with other social institutions and eventually these institutions lose their reason for being. The earlier view finds the cause in theological, philosophical and sociological factors ebbing and flowing over the past

3,000 years. It is the evolution of society from one cultural form to another. Those who argue that the cause is socialism suggest that the solution is to return to the past when the State's role was more limited. Sorokin, on the other hand, tends to take a more cyclical view of history and concludes that society is experiencing a natural evolution towards an alternative form.

These positions, both from the twentieth century, are only a partial picture. Looking back further still to the turn of the century, a considerable amount of evidence was presented to the Royal Commission on the Poor Laws and Relief of Distress that emphasizes the same perceived crisis[10]. The testimony had a familiar ring: 'the disinclination of relatives to assist one another'. It was further charged that 'there is not the same disposition to assist one another that there was years ago'. But how many years ago were they speaking of? In the Report of the Royal Commission of 1832, seventy years earlier, we find the following:

It appears from the whole Evidence that the clause of the 43rd Eliz., which directs the parents and children of the impotent to be assessed for their support, is very seldom enforced. In any ordinary state of society, we much doubt the wisdom of such an enactment. The duty of supporting parents and children in old age or infirmity is so strongly enforced by our natural feelings, that it is well performed, even among savages, and almost always so in a nation deserving the name of civilized. We believe that England is the only European country in which it is neglected[11].

What conclusions can be drawn from this retracing of the past 150 years? Perhaps one is that people in each successive generation when confronted with some crisis invariably looked at the family as it then existed, disliked what they saw, and suggested that the deterioration could only be reversed if families became more like those of the past. Another is that each generation might have held up too high an ideal. While the conclusions were similar, the same cannot be said for the perceived cause of the deterioration. Some saw the reasons as spiritual (attributable to religion or its absence); others as biological (a regression towards the mean resulting in the inevitable deterioration of the human stock) or physical (sun spots or climactic shifts). The most recurring argument sees the cause in socio-political factors and in turn both capitalism and socialism have received their share of the blame.

Thus present concerns are not unique to this time. As a theme, it can be found in generations preceding the nineteenth century. It would be extremely difficult and somewhat immaterial to this study to trace the evolution back to that period where a generation would flatly state that their position was better than previous eras and then measure the actual or perceived 'deterioration' up to the present. The evidence, however, does suggest that large numbers of people have been and are convinced that family deterioration has occurred and it disturbs them. The recent wave of nostalgia about life in the past and family life in particular are particularly good examples of this. The media, the theatre and literature have glorified the past. It was a better time to live, life was less complex, and appropriate values were respected. Since each generation appears to have reached the same conclusion, one has to question whether they are speaking of a past they knew, one that they imagine, or a past they need to believe existed even if it never did.

Schorr perhaps has made the most reasoned statement on this issue when he suggested:

The flat statement that the family ... is deteriorating cannot be supported. The family is changing. Some of the changes may be bad, and others are all to the good. As far as the relations of older men and women and their children are concerned, to say that the net effect is on the debit side is a distortion[12].

This is the key. All social institutions change, the family among them. The need, then, is to analyse this change and its social policy implications. In the case of the family and the care of the socially dependent, it is of little value to suggest a return to the past. Today's society is not yesterday's. Read Dickens, Rowntree, Booth or Engels, with their vivid descriptions of massive poverty, alienation and staggering morbidity and mortality rates. There have been significant improvements in the overall quality of life. In turn, these improvements have conceivably created new demands on families, demands which previous families were not required to meet. For example, it is possible that families today have been forced to, or are expected to, assume a caring function for the frail elderly and the severely handicapped child simply because the elderly and the severely handicapped child are surviving in greater numbers.

The family and the State: the nature of the relationship

This chapter began with the statement that the structure of the Welfare State depends on a set of assumptions concerning the responsibilities which families are expected to carry for the care of the socially dependent and a set of conditions under which this responsibility is to be shared or taken over by society. This implies that the family as an institution functions as a social service in the care of the socially dependent, and that society, through its organized social welfare system, also has a role. The question was then raised whether the caring function should be shared by both and if so, how each social institution should relate to the other. If the State is, in fact, assuming more responsibility, and families less, are there identifiable boundaries to this shift?

A number of different dimensions of this relationship can be identified. In paradigm form it can be categorized as either a complete or partial transfer, permanent or temporary. A third dimension would discriminate between social welfare services that support the family or substitute for it in its function as a social service. The value of such an approach to the analysis of this policy issue is not in the development of a matrix of discrete categories into which specific policies could be placed, but rather that themes might be identified, themes that bear on the family, how the family views the social welfare system, and more importantly, how the State views the family.

For example, a large number of the elderly are residing in various types of institutional settings and it is likely that they will be there until they die. The transfer in this case is complete and permanent, and the social welfare system in providing total care has substituted for the family. An example in which the transfer is complete but temporary and one which could be described as supporting the family would be the provision of short-term institutional care for a mentally handicapped child or an aged person. In the first example, the State becomes the family in so far as it assumes certain functions; in the second, the State supports the family by providing some relief. While complete transfer will invariably mean some form of institutionalization, the form of the transfer, whether it is permanent or temporary, whether its intent is to take over from or to complement the family, can have significantly different outcomes.

Most of the community-based services have evolved on the principle that it is often (though not always) in the best interest of the family and the handicapped member if the family were to retain the major responsibility for the caring function. It is also recognized that the family benefits if society provides some element of the care. The development of the home help services, meals on wheels, the deployment of health visitors and social workers, are all examples of a partial transfer and depending on the nature of the specific situation can be provided on either a temporary or permanent basis.

Of major concern to this study is whether existing social policies, regardless of the scope or time scale involved, substitute for or complement the family. Are the domiciliary services in practice given to the socially dependent only when the family cannot or will not provide care (the supplementary or residual approach), or are they used to strengthen families who are quite willing to carry the primary caring function? Policies based on the concept of substitution suggest that the relationship between the family and the social welfare system is exclusive (either/or) while policies that emphasize a complementary function assume an interdependency. This latter approach implicitly argues that the family needs the intervention of society and that the social welfare system needs the family, since the social and economic costs are too great for either to carry alone. We need only to look at social welfare expenditures over the past twenty years to appreciate this fact. Between 1953 and 1972 the gross domestic product (GDP) in constant prices rose by 68 per cent; public expenditure increased by 83 per cent; and social welfare expenditure, representing almost half of all public expenditure (see Table 5.2, p. 99), grew by 139 per cent, most important, expenditure in the personal social services, as one component of social welfare grew by almost 400 per cent[13]. Speculate what would happen if the family were to transfer more and more responsibility to the State for the care of the socially dependent and the handicapped in particular, and if the demand were for social welfare provisions that took over from rather than supported the family. It would take but a small shift of this kind to bring about a greater economic crisis. For example, data from the General Household Survey [14] show that in a one-month reference period, slightly over 2 per cent of the general population used one or more of the basic health and welfare domiciliary services. Turning to high risk groups, in 1974 less than 3 per cent of the elderly were living in institutions (homes for the elderly, nursing homes and mental hospitals); under 4 per cent regularly received meals either in their own homes or in clubs and centres; between 6 and 7 per cent received home helps in the course of the year and about 10 per cent were visited by a home nurse. Less than 30 per cent of severely mentally handicapped children were institutionalized on a more or less permanent basis. It is exceedingly difficult to attempt to put a cost figure on the care provided by families. Young and Willmott, using calculations from C. Clark, estimated that if married men were to pay their wives as housekeepers, the estimated cost would be £20,000 million[15]. If the State were to pay families who cared for their handicapped members a sum equal to the cost of care in institutions, or even the current rate paid to homemakers, the costs to the public sector would be staggering.

Plan of the study

This study has set out to examine this reliance on the family and to determine whether there were shifts in practice on the part of families and professionals engaged in the development, delivery or consumption of social welfare services. The questions that have been raised throughout this chapter are difficult to analyse, let alone answer, and it is not surprising that there is no set methodology that can be applied. Rather than beginning with the collection of new data (for example through a large-scale survey) it was decided that a more efficient and productive approach might be the analysis of existing information. The very nature of the issue requires that the study be exploratory, and a major objective is to generate hypotheses relevant to policy. The results of this work include an analysis of past and current trends in what families seek, what services are provided, and the implications of these trends for future policy. Specific areas are: the social service function of families with handicapped members; the supports required by the non-handicapped members of the family; and the function of the organized social welfare system. The methodology arrived at is in keeping with the idea of an exploratory study and two primary sources are employed: existing data bases and a series of interviews with relevant practitioners in the field.

Analysis of available data　Three major categories of data were examined dealing with:

1. the family;
2. mentally handicapped children and handicapped elderly;
3. families providing care to these two groups.

Under the family, a number of themes are explored. The first is the conceptual issue of the purposes of the family, specifically the socialization, economic and personal care functions. A second theme examines the evolution of family types as this affects its ability to carry out these functions. Both required a review of available sociological and anthropological literature. A third theme deals with the delineation of socio-economic factors that affect the social service function of the family; here the major data sources used are the General Census and the General Household Survey.

In dealing with the other two categories, the concern is with identifying prevalence data, need estimates and service provision. Primary sources included various surveys undertaken by the government, voluntary organizations and individual researchers, as well as specific research studies dealing with families with handicapped members.

Interviews   To go beyond the data, the facts and estimates which are tied primarily to existing policies and programmes, and to explore the less clear area (in the sense of documentation) of the family as a resource, the family requiring resources, and the transfer of responsibility, a significant number of interviews were carried out with representatives of various organizations. These included national voluntary organizations, the Department of Health and Social Security, individual researchers and academicians, and families. In addition, extended visits were made to four local authorities in London, the Midlands, the Yorkshire area and Wales. These interviews were used to explore with a cross-section of policy makers, planners and administrators, and front-line practitioners, their impressions of the strengths and deficiencies of the existing system and their ideas of desirable policy development.

Visits were also made to two other countries, Denmark and the Federal Republic of Germany to gain some understanding of their general policy approach to the issue of family—State relationships in the care of the handicapped. While the data analysis in the study is specific to the United Kingdom, it was felt that the experiences of these countries, combined with the author's working knowledge of the American pattern, might provide an additional frame of reference for the discussion of future policy evolution. It was further assumed that given this perspective, the findings might have wider applicability.

The rest of the report discusses what was found. Chapter 2 explores the concept of the family as a primary social service, Chapters 3 and 4 provide descriptive material of two at risk groups, their characteristics and needs, and how the social welfare system has been organized to assist them and their families. The idea of a caring society, both its quantitative and qualitative aspects, is introduced in Chapter 5, and finally, in Chapter 6, the initial policy questions are re-examined and implications for policy and practice and research discussed.

References

1. A number of writers have attempted to clarify this issue. See: R. Titmuss, *Commitment to Welfare*, Allen and Unwin, 1968; M. Rein, *Social Policy: Issues of Choice and Change*, New York, Random House, 1970; D. Gil, *Unravelling Social Policy*, Cambridge, Shankman, 1973; T. H. Marshall, *Social Policy*, Hutchinson, 1967.

2. See N. Cohen, *Social Work and Social Problems*, New York, National Association of Social Workers, 1964, pp. ix—xiv for an informative discussion of what constitutes a social problem.

3. Both M. Rein and D. Donnison touch on this issue. M. Rein, 'Social policy analyses as the interpretation of beliefs', *Journal of the American Institute of Planners*, September 1971; D. Donnison, 'Ideologies and policy', *Journal of Social Policy*, 1, 2, 1972, 97—117.

4. The phrase 'Welfare State' is used more in an ideological sense than as a description of a specific set of policies and programmes that could be used to differentiate a Welfare State from a non-welfare State or to locate individual societies on a Welfare State continuum. It refers to the gradual evolution of some societies from periods characterized by *laissez-faire* and little or minimal governmental intervention to periods when the State accepts increased responsibility for meeting basic human needs. The term 'social welfare' as used in this context refers to the particular set of instrumentalities that a particular society develops to fulfil the goals of the Welfare State, and social services are seen as the specific programmes.

5. For an elaboration of this issue see: R. Titmuss, op. cit. (ref. 1); H. Wilensky and C. Lebeaux, *Industrial Society and Social Welfare*, New York, The Free Press, 1965 (especially Ch. 6); and M. Rein, op. cit. (ref. 1).

6. For example, see: *Social Insurance and Allied Services*, HMSO, Cmd 6404, 1942; the National Assistance Act 1948 and the National Health Service Act, 1946; the Mental Health Act 1959; *Better Services for the Mentally Handicapped*, HMSO, Cmnd 4683, 1971.

7. Sir Keith Joseph, 'Britain: A decadent new Utopia', *The Guardian*, 21 October 1974.

8. M. Rein, op. cit. (ref. 3), pp. 297—310.

9. Pitrim A. Sorokin, *The Crisis of our Age*, New York, Dutton, 1946, p. 188; pp. 190—1.

10. *Report of the Royal Commission on the Poor Laws and Relief of Distress*, Cd 4499, 1909. While the entire Report is replete with examples of their concern for family responsibility, see especially Vol. II, Ch. 3 of Pt VIII, 'Recovery of cost of relief'.

11. *Report of the Poor Law Commission of 1832*, Cd 2728, 1905, p. 43.

12. Alvin Schorr, 'Beyond pluck and luck' in *Explorations in Social Policy*, New York, Basic Books, 1968, p. 133.

13. Admittedly expenditures in the personal social services have been increased from a small base. They merit special attention, however, following the report of the Seebohm Committee. 'We are convinced that if local authorities are to provide an effective family service they must assume wider responsibilities than they have at the present for the prevention, treatment and relief of social problems. . . . Much more ought to be done, for example, for the very old and the under fives, for physically and mentally handicapped', *Report of the Committee on Local Authority and Allied Personal Social Services*, Cmnd 3703, HMSO, 1969, Ch. VII.

14. OPCS, Social Survey Division, *General Household Survey*, HMSO, 1973, p. 334.

15. M. Young and P. Willmott, *The Symmetrical Family*, Routledge and Kegan Paul, 1973, p. 110; C. Clark, 'The economics of housework', *Bulletin of the Oxford Institute of Statistics*, **20**, no. 2, 1958, 205–11.

2 The family and the caring function

In the preceding chapter the general policy issue was introduced and a number of questions raised related to concerns and ambiguities surrounding the nature of the relationship between the family and the organized social welfare system. It was pointed out that there has been an increased transfer of the caring function to the State and that this shift may have affected the family's capacity and perceived role in meeting the needs of its physically and mentally handicapped members. Still there have been few systematic studies of this critical social policy issue.

Are there reasonable boundaries to this transfer, boundaries that capitalize on some form of partnership or are previous patterns changing? If there are shifts in practice what are the implications for social policy? What are the social and economic costs involved and is society willing or capable of meeting them? In this chapter, one dimension of the question is explored, the role of the family as a social service[1].

Functions of the family

It is impossible to offer many generalizations or universal statements about the family that some authority will not challenge. While one expert argues that the family as a social institution is not only dissolving but has actually become an anachronism[2], another applauds its state of health[3] and a third maintains that though there might be some changes in family structure, eventually it will evolve into a more viable form[4]. Each position is accompanied by an impressive array of data. Each conclusion is credible if the reader is willing to accept each authority's implicit definition of what a family is and what it should be.

The single proposition that might be allowed to stand unscathed is that all societies have been characterized by some form of family structure and this unit usually carried out certain key functions. While the form of the structure, the specific ways by which the family fulfilled these functions, and the extent to which they were shared with other institutions has changed over time, there has always been, in recorded history, some basic social unit that could be called a family.

Whether family life was natural or created in the sense of a social contract is largely a matter of speculation. Regardless of how it came into being, as an institution it was more capable of achieving the survival needs of its individual members than they could on their own. These basic needs included both physical and social needs and specific family functions are usually described as procreation, protection, social control and socialization, physical and emotional care.

Where there were families, in time there were associations of families or communities held together by common interests. Additional institutions were created, capable of providing a wider range of basic services on a much more efficient and effective scale. Whether families lived in hunting, agrarian or industrial societies, they were probably never totally self-sufficient. While previous societies may have been less complex, while the network of social relations may have been more informal, families have shared these basic functions with extra-familial institutions[5]. Sussman brings out this idea of the family sharing these basic social functions with other institutions when he defines the functions of the family 'developing their [members] capacities to socialize children, enhancing the competence of their members to cope with the demands of other organizations in which they must function, utilizing these organizations, and providing the satisfactions and a healthy environment to the well-being of a family'[6].

The relevant question then becomes one of delineating those functions more appropriate for the family to undertake, those that are more appropriate for other institutions, and those that are to be shared. Social scientists over the first half of this century took the position that there was minimal sharing and that the family had been pressured into surrendering most of their functions to other social institutions. Despite the fact that research over the past twenty years has seriously questioned this conclusion, a significant number of those who are responsible for shaping social policies, administering programmes and delivering services, tend to operate on this earlier assumption. Since their actions have considerable impact on families, it is useful to sketch the argument and the factors associated with the position. It was charged that initially the family lost its economic function to the industrial sector, leaving it with the residual functions of reproduction and the care of the socially dependent — children, the old and the sick. Industrial society created a family structure more suited to its needs than earlier forms which were likely to be characterized as more complete economic and political units composed of a number of sub-families, whose needs were met through an interdependent extended kin system[7].

While this concept of the extended family must be viewed as an ideal type rather than an empirical description of all pre-industrial families it does provide a number of insights. The extended family was large, it was both a production and consumption unit, and to some extent was relatively self-sufficient. Better suited to a farming society, it became unnecessary and counterproductive to a highly mechanized labour market. The extended family, unable to adjust to these new pressures, gradually disintegrated and a new structure, the nuclear family, gradually evolved. This new unit, composed of husband, wife and children, independent from their kin-related families, was viewed as 'the ideal structure for meeting the demands of geographical and occupational mobility, such mobility being prerequisite to successful performance in modern industrial society'[8].

The nuclear family evolved precisely because it met the criteria of efficiency and effectiveness required by the economic system. As with any major shifts or changes there were bound to be casualties and in the absence of the extended care network, society accepted the responsibility of developing an infrastructure of formal social organizations to provide care for those unable to adjust. Those functions, previously carried out by families, were still viewed as important, but other institutions were judged to be more capable of undertaking them.

Earlier it was pointed out that the family was viewed as retaining certain residual functions: procreation, some elements of socialization, and the care of the dependent. In fact, these functions were not 'family' functions but were, more often than not, the responsibility of the women in the family. In time, these too were affected as larger numbers of mothers entered the labour force. The socialization of children was seen as a function that legitimately should be shared with other institutions. Examples of these are the introduction of compulsory education towards the end of the nineteenth century and the recent expansion of formal day-care programmes.

The process of birth and the care of the sick and infirm became the responsibility of the health system, leaving, it was argued, minimal socialization and recreational functions to the family. And now these developments, initiated over 150 years ago, have created a situation that many feel is serious. Families, either willingly or under external pressure, have given up many of the functions traditionally carried out by families and by seeking support for their members from other social institutions have become dependent on these institutions and the State. The idea of shared responsibility is no longer viable in presentday society since the family has little to share.

While this analysis has been outlined in somewhat exaggerated terms, it does capture the essence of the argument. Has the extended family disappeared as many social scientists have tended to believe and many policy makers, planners and administrators still believe? Is the nuclear family *the* dominant family structure, and what is it about the nuclear family that would minimize its ability to provide care for its dependent members, especially the physically and mentally handicapped?

Characteristics of the modern family

Families today differ significantly from those of the nineteenth century and some of these differences potentially affect a family's capability and willingness to provide effective social care for their dependent members. This section examines some of the more critical changes. Perhaps the most notable is the size of the family itself. In the middle of the nineteenth century the average family had seven children. A hundred years later this number had shrunk to slightly over two, a reduction of two-thirds. Even though women were marrying younger in each successive generation and theoretically were likely to have more children, the birth rate has dropped significantly from 1900 to 1950. While the birth rate did swing upwards in

1960, it has begun to fall again in the 1970s. Since 1920 the norm for most families seems to be two or fewer children, reaching a peak between 1930 and 1940 when seven out of ten families fell into this category.

Table 2.1   *Family size 1860—1970, England and Wales*

Year of marriage	Average age of female at marriage	Average number of children	Birth rate per 1,000 population	Per cent families with two or fewer children
1860	27	7.0	—	—
1880	27	6.0	—	—
1900	25.6	4.0	28.7	—
1910	25.6	3.0	24.5	—
1920	25.5	2.4	22.8	64.0
1930	25.5	2.1	15.8	69.0
1940	25.0	2.1	15.9	69.0
1950	24.6	(2.3)	15.5	(63.0)
1960	23.3	—	17.1	(61.0)
1970	22.6	—	16.0	—

Note: Figures in brackets are based mainly on actual data but in part on assumptions underlying the 1972-based population projections.

Sources: GSS, *Social Trends*, HMSO, 1974, pp. 76—8; and *Annual Abstract of Statistics*, HMSO, 1972, p. 30; P. R. Cox, *Demography*, 4th edn, Cambridge University Press, 1970, p. 345.

This trend in fertility and its effect on family structure has had a significant impact on family life. In 1850 the average mother was still bearing children well into her thirties, whereas her counterpart 100 years later had completed her child-bearing functions in her mid-twenties[9]. As Titmuss pointed out:

It would seem that the typical working-class mother of the 1890s, married in her teens or early twenties, and experiencing ten pregnancies, spent about fifteen years in a state of pregnancy and in nursing a child for the first year of its life. She was tied for this period of time, to the wheel of child bearing. Today, for the typical mother, the time so spent would be about four years[10].

Young and Willmott commenting on this argue that 'the mother's last child (1890s) would not have left school until she was in her mid-fifties, by which time she would be as active all over again in her role of grandmother'[11]. The presentday mother is likely to have completed her child-rearing functions in her forties.

There are any number of reasons offered to explain these changes. One theory is that the more industrialized a society becomes, the greater the rate of decline in family size[12]. A number of factors are usually identified as associated with this. It has been suggested that as society becomes more industrialized it develops some form of social security system. Without such a system parents, however erroneously, viewed their children as their social insurance for old age and the greater the number of children, the greater the insurance. As collective social insurance mechanisms become available, the perceived need ceases. A second possible factor was the gradual reduction of mortality rates in general, particularly of infant mortality. In an agricultural society children had an economic value. When infant mortality rates were high the norm was to have a large number of children on the assumption that only a small number would survive. Even after these mortality rates decreased, the majority of families continued to have a large number of children and it was only in this century that the time lag has closed. Related to this transition is the argument that children are less valuable in an industrial society than in agrarian societies. If they begin work at an early age they are in competition with adults, if they remain in school they are unproductive consumers of family income. Large families are seen as drawbacks to upward social mobility. A fourth reason was the non-availability and/or non-reliability of fertility control methods. The final factor is that the role and expectations of women have changed. In the past women had few opportunities for a career outside the home. Since the Second World War, not only have more opportunities for outside employment opened up but women have been encouraged for economic reasons to limit the number of children in their families. Large families, highly desirable in the past, have come to be seen as a hindrance to social mobility and a high standard of living.

Mothers, having completed their child-bearing functions earlier than their predecessors, saw that they had roughly thirty years more of productive life before they became classified as elderly. For a growing number this meant paid employment.

Table 2.2 *Female participation rate in the work force, 1921–91, England and Wales*

Year	Per cent women working	Per cent married women working	Married women as per cent of total work force
1921	32.3	8.7	3.8
1931	34.2	10.0	4.5
1951	34.7	26.1	13.7
1961	37.5	34.0	18.0
1971	42.7	40.9	22.5
1976	43.0	44.3	25.0
1981	44.0	46.2	26.0
1991	44.6	47.5	26.9

Sources: British Labour Statistics, *Historical Abstracts 1886–1968*, Table 109, 1971; Census of Population 1971, *Economic Activity Table*, Part 1; *Department of Employment Gazette*, 1974.

In 1921 one out of every three women, but less than one in ten married women, were in the work force. Over the next twenty years there was little change in these rates but during the war years the number of married women working increased sharply. Initially it was felt that many of these women would return to the home after the crisis was over, but experience since then clearly shows that married women have become a permanent part of the labour pool. Over the past twenty-five years the number has been increasing steadily and if present trends continue it is estimated that about one-half of all married women will be working by 1991. Even now the number of married women in the work force is greater than the number of single women (3.9 million compared to 3.2 million) and as of 1971 the ratio was five to three[13]. The reasons married women work are complex and varied. More and more are doing so to achieve a sense of self-fulfilment; many work because they have become the main provider for their families. Most women, however, work to supplement family income. As the standard of living rose and many goods previously viewed as luxuries became accessible, expectations and demand increased. Family income derived from two sources became a necessity for most. The opportunities were there and married women were no longer tied down by large families, long years of child rearing, and exclusionary labour force practices[14]. To some extent there has been a return to pre-industrial family life where both parents were working.

And yet this freedom was only temporary and many families found themselves faced with an uncomfortable dilemma. While it is true that much of the caring function was reduced, as there were fewer children, the overall dependency ratio has not changed in over 120 years. The composition, of course, has.

Table 2.3   *Dependency ratio, 1851–1971, England and Wales*

Year	Per cent 0–14	Per cent elderly	Dependency ratio
1851	35.6	5.9	415
1901	32.5	6.2	387
1951	23.3	16.5	398
1971	23.9	16.4	403

Notes: 1. Per cent elderly: for males, sixty-five years of age and over; for females, sixty years of age and over. 2. Dependency ratio is defined as the ratio of the population 0–14 years of age and the elderly per 1,000 total population.

Sources: Census of Population, 1971: *Age, Marital Condition and General Tables*, Table 5.

During the nineteenth century and early years of the twentieth, dependants were largely children. As the birth rate decreased and longevity increased more and more of the population moved into old age. The dependent population took on a new shape. In 1851 the elderly made up only 14 per cent of the dependent population; by 1951, 100 years later, they constituted a remarkable 41 per cent. For every six dependant children there were four people classified as elderly. Children were no longer making most of the demands on the family, now they are sharing them with their grandparents. This trend is expected to continue throughout the rest of this century. The dependency ratio itself will fluctuate between 384 and 386, a slight drop from 1971, but the elderly will make up between 42 and 45 per cent[15].

Families, especially mothers, are faced with new pressures, since it is not a matter of simply transferring the care from their children to elderly parents. For most families there is a considerable hiatus in years. As discussed earlier, mothers were able to complete their child-bearing functions in their mid-twenties and were in their early thirties when the children went to school. Fifteen to twenty years later the new dependent group, their aged parents, required care. Furthermore, the type of care required was not the same as that needed by their children.

Previously this had created fewer problems. There were fewer aged and when a family did have aged members, some family member was usually available to provide care. Few mothers worked and, more important, many families had unmarried daughters or other relatives living with them. Theoretically this group, especially those between the ages of forty-five and sixty, were the caretakers as they are the generation immediately preceding the elderly group. This does not mean that the caring persons were always female and always middle-aged. There is considerable evidence that people over sixty-five years of age are caring for their own elderly parents who are in their eighties or nineties and in a significant number of instances grandchildren provide assistance and support[16].

This pool of potential caretakers has shrunk over the past fifty years. Over half of the married women between the ages of forty-five and sixty were employed in 1971, compared to less than 10 per cent in 1921. The shift first appeared in the 1940s, accelerated in the 1950s and early 1960s, and exploded in the last five years. What is even more significant is that currently, married women in this age group are more likely to be working than married women in any other age group, with the result that they have become either increasingly unavailable to care for the family's dependent members or they are finding it necessary to carry out this function as well as work outside the house.

Table 2.4   *Per cent married women aged 45–60 in the work force, 1921–71, England and Wales*

Age group	1921	1931	1951	1961	1966	1971
45–54	8.4	8.5	23.7	36.1	49.8	57.0
55–59	–	7.0	15.6	26.4	38.4	45.5

Source: Department of Employment, *Women at Work: a statistical survey*, Manpower Paper no. 9, HMSO, 1974, p. 44.

The caretaker ratio developed in Table 2.5 is built on two potential sources of care: married and single women between the ages of forty-five and sixty. In 1901, for every 100 elderly persons in the general popula-tion, there were eighty-three women aged forty-five to fifty-nine, of whom thirteen were single, almost a one to one ratio. Fifty years later this ratio had dropped sharply and by 1971 it had been halved. While the number of women forty-five to sixty had increased from 6 to 8 per cent (keeping in mind that the majority are working) the number of elderly grew from less than 8 to 19 per cent. Shifts among single women in this age group are even more striking. Whereas there were thirteen spinsters (1901) for every 100 elderly, now there are only five. Shifts in marital status have been sharp since the war. Approximately 14 per cent of all women between forty-five and sixty were unmarried in 1901. By 1971 only 8 per cent were unmarried. The caretaker pool has been effectively reduced by demo-graphic changes (shifts in age structure and marital status) and competing demands on time.

Table 2.5   *Caretaker pool 1901—71, United Kingdom*

Year	Per cent total pop. elderly	Per cent women 45—59	Rate/ 1,000 elderly	Per cent single women 45—59	Rate/1,000 elderly
1901	7.6	6.3	830	0.8	130
1911	8.1	6.9	850	1.1	160
1921	9.8	8.2	840	1.3	160
1931	11.3	9.1	810	1.5	160
1951	17.0	9.5	640	1.5	110
1961	18.7	9.3	610	1.3	90
1971	19.0	8.1	490	0.8	50

Note: Percentages were derived by dividing the numbers in these age groups by the total (male and female) population.

Sources: Social Trends, 1971 and 1974.

Another characteristic of the modern industrial family is the high degree of geographic mobility. The economic system required a highly mobile unit, unhindered, and able to change residence often and easily. While trend data is difficult to obtain, the modern family appears to have adjusted to this requirement. Between 1958 and 1963 slightly more than three out of every ten persons over the age of fifteen had moved within the previous five years (31.6 per cent); between 1966 and 1971 this percentage had increased to 35.7 per cent. More than a third of the adult population thus moves every five years. From 1960 to 1971 between 7 and 9 per cent moved every year[17], and of these almost half were considerable distances[18]. This represents a noticeable increase from the decade of the 1950s when the percentage of those who moved from their town or borough was less than 4 per cent on an annual basis[19]. Not every population group moves to the same degree and migration patterns are highly correlated with social class, income and age. Moves have been affected by changes in employment, marital status, and demands for more appropriate housing[20].

If social mobility is positively related to geographic mobility, the family that wants to or has to provide care for the socially dependent, especially the handicapped is at a distinct disadvantage. While physical relocation can be seen as causing some family disruption, for these families the move can be a major crisis. The elderly are usually more reluctant to move from familiar environments and their families are faced with difficult choices. The problem is probably even more difficult in families where there are handicapped children. If physical adaptations have been made to the home the family must be prepared to begin all over again. Contacts with hospitals, clinics and social agencies providing services to families have to be broken and the process of finding the necessary supports re-instituted. Given these considerations not all families can move freely and yet geographical mobility is becoming the norm of modern society.

Closely associated with the phenomenon of mobility is the question of availability and type of housing. Both surveys cited above stress that almost half of all moves are related to housing or employment. Many families find their housing too small for their needs, others lack basic amenities. A third group are forced to move when they find it impossible to find reasonably priced housing in their area. While the present housing situation is described as one of the most serious current social problems facing the country, it is fair to say that it has been one for the past seventy years. Since the First World War successive governments have made housing a priority area. Between the wars, more than 4.5 million houses and flats were built in England and Wales, one-third by the local government. Over the past twenty-five years this ratio has shifted considerably and 56 per cent of all houses and flats were built by local authorities.

Table 2.6   *Permanent housing completed 1945–73, England and Wales*

Period	Per cent local authority	Per cent 4 or more bedrooms	Per cent private owners	Per cent 4 or more bedrooms	Total completions (000's)
1945–59	66.9	2.4	33.1	3.5	3,042
1960–64	62.1	2.0	37.9	3.8	1,424
1965–69	43.6	2.6	56.4	6.4	1,744
1970–73	37.8	4.1	62.2	10.4	1,125

Sources: A. H. Halsey, ed., *Trends in British Society Since 1900*, Macmillan, 1972, p. 311; Department of the Environment, *Housing and Construction Statistics*, no. 12, 1969, and no. 8, 1973.

While the commitment on the public sector has been considerable, it is still viewed as inadequate. Regardless of the problem of scale, the form of the development has had an impact on family life. Of the more than 7,300,000 flats and houses completed, less than 300,000 (4 per cent) had four or more bedrooms. Large families and three generation families wanting to live in the same household have tremendous difficulties in finding adequate homes. Even this figure of 4 per cent is misleading, as most of the larger homes were built by the private sector (over two-thirds), while only 2.5 per cent of all public sector completions were houses or flats with at least four bedrooms. Private sector housing was much more expensive and a considerable number of families were and are dependent on local authority housing. In practice then the State's housing policy recognized the small nuclear family to be the dominant family type. Since 1960, ninety-six of every one hundred houses and flats completed by local authorities have been one to three bedroom homes. This by no means implies that the State explicitly set out to shape the structure of the family. It may have, but the converse is equally probable — the State might merely have responded to smaller family units.

Implications of these changes for families

It is clear then that there have been significant changes in family structure over the past 100 years. Families are smaller and more likely to be characterized as units of husband, wife and offspring (nuclear families) or of husband and wife alone without children or no children living at home (nuclear dyads). The norm is for both husband and wife to be employed, the latter after a relatively short period of child-bearing and rearing. Families change their residences frequently with a considerable degree of moving from one area to another. Finally, the housing stock reflects these changes and houses and flats are likely to be one or two bedroom units. All these changes probably influenced the earlier social scientists to conclude that the traditional extended family has dissolved, and that where it did exist it was an anomaly. The nuclear family, small, isolated but more self-sufficient than its predecessor, was seen as the dominant form. Consequently it was argued that the family could no longer function as the primary resource for many of the socially dependent but found it necessary to transfer this caring role to other social institutions. It was inevitable and rational, and its implications should be taken into account by those responsible for the formulation of social policies and the planning of social welfare programmes.

Although it is impossible to deny these changes in family structure, it is another matter to agree with some of the above conclusions. While it might be more difficult for the modern family to function as a social service, is there evidence to support the conclusion that it has ceased to do so? Sussman's position is interesting:

The theoretical position assumed ... is that there exists in modern urban industrial societies . . . an extended kin family system, highly integrated within a network of social relationships and mutual assistance, that operates along bi-lateral kin lines and vertically over several generations. The validity of this position is established by the accumulation of empirical evidence on the structure and functioning of urban kin networks . . . [evidence] so convincing that we find it unnecessary to continue further descriptive work in order to establish . . . [its] existence [21].

His conclusion that the extended family not only still exists but has demonstrated a strong capacity for mutual support as a unit is fully supported by data from other Western countries[22]. While they agree that the traditional extended family, characterized by interdependent sub-family units, has broken down they argue that the evolution has been not to the isolated nuclear unit, but to a modified extended family structure 'which consists of a coalition of nuclear families in a state of partial dependence'[23]. Significant services are exchanged though the individual family units retain a high degree of autonomy. But why have these differences of opinion emerged? Sussman suggests that many of the earlier sociologists viewed the world in dichotomies or binaries. Families were thus likely to be characterized as either extended or nuclear units[24]. Another possible explanation is that early sociologists developed their theories when the prevalence of three-generational families was low. For example, from 1851 to 1901 less than 5 per cent of the total population were over sixty-four years of age and it was only in 1951 that the percentage exceeded 10 per cent[25]. At the turn of the century, for every one hundred families there were only twenty-five aged persons; by 1931 there were thirty aged persons and by 1971 there were forty-five elderly. Sociologists were thus observing the modal two-generation family. A final contributory factor was probably the fallacy of equating the nuclear household with the nuclear family. There can be little argument that the classical extended family of sub-family units living together or in very close proximity has dissolved. There is disagreement, however, that this has resulted in an inevitable breakdown of the kin network. Furthermore, it is not clear whether earlier forms of family structure were more capable of providing needed care for their dependent members.

It was pointed out earlier that during the transition from an agricultural to an industrial society there were bound to be casualties. The traditional extended family was non-functional, but the isolated nuclear family was probably as ineffective in meeting the new pressures. Anderson seems to support this notion of a period of uncertainty for families and suggests that the extended family actually became more viable in this century[26].

. . . it was probably only after the introduction of the old age pension had transferred much of the economic burden of old age from kin . . . that a really strong affective and non-calculative commitment to the kinship net could develop and 'traditional' community solidarity become possible.

The nineteenth-century family, particularly three-generational families, had only the Poor Law institution to look to for assistance and for a number of families this was either an unacceptable alternative or they could not meet the strict eligibility criteria[27]. Dependants were kept in the family but often at a high cost in both material and interpersonal well-being, and testimony from the 1909 Royal Commission attacks the myth of the role and status of dependents in nineteenth-century family life

The large majority of those who endure biting poverty without seeking relief from the Guardians are women. Men do not so frequently attain to old age under disadvantageous circumstances as women do. Old men go more readily into the Workhouse than old women. Women struggle longer and with greater determination with the difficulties of poverty and the incapacities of old age. Families in poor circumstances find it less possible to provide food and shelter for an old man who is a relative than for an old woman. He is more in the way, he expects not only a larger portion of the food, but to share in the better portions. He does not fit into the household of a working family as an old woman does and is not so useful in domestic matters. His welcome is colder. . . . A decent old woman will cling to a home where she may be regarded as a drudge . . . and she will exist on the plainer portions of the meals and will wedge in both day and night without encroaching much on the means of the family[28].

This is precisely the point that Anderson and Rosenheim emphasized. Where there were three-generational families (a form of the extended family) in the last century, the living conditions for most of the elderly were probably low. Care was provided to the old and handicapped but what kind of care? Was it offered freely and with affection or was it perceived as something that had to be done? Conceivably, the early developments of the Welfare State in this century had a positive effect on the family and contrary to the arguments of some social critics, strengthened family life. By removing the economic strain and establishing an income maintenance floor, family members were finally capable of providing other forms of support.

Families and the provision of social care

The argument that the dominant form of family structure is not the nuclear family but the modified extended family is based on a number of facts: the existence of three-generational families, the amount of vertical and horizontal communication between family sub-units, and the extent to which family members offer assistance to each other. While it is difficult to draw conclusions about the quality of these interactions from quantitative data, it is safe to say that high interaction is a necessary condition for emotional closeness.

That the three-generational family is a dominant form of family structure is indisputable. What causes some concern to many professionals is that the majority of old people do not live with their children. This pattern has been offered as evidence that the elderly are neglected by their children and living in virtual social isolation. Rather than a form of the extended family, the multi-generational family is in practice two or more isolated nuclear units whose only common bond is biological.

Shanas and others over the past fifteen to twenty years have been attacking this conclusion. Interestingly she argues that the conclusion comes from two sources, old people who are childless themselves and professionals engaged in providing services to the aged. Old people who are isolated, who either have not had children or whose children are not supportive, tend to generalize from their unique situation to all elderly persons. The professionals on their part possibly lose sight of the fact that they come into contact primarily with those elderly who are in need, who have problems, whose family have withdrawn support. What Shanas and others suggest is that these are a minority[29].

The elderly do live alone but usually by choice. Their preference is to live near their families but not with them[30]. A large body of research over the past fifteen years has carefully documented the extent to which there is intergenerational contact and mutual support. The major part of this reciprocal help appears to be related to class. Lower income groups provide physical care, household help, childminding and recreation while middle income groups tend to help financially[31]. On the basis of these data it is clear that at least through the 1960s, a dominant form of family structure in this country was the modified extended unit and a recent national survey of the elderly suggests it still exists[32]. The World Health Organization has taken the position that:

wherever careful studies have been carried out in the industrialized countries, the lasting devotion of children for their parents has been amply demonstrated. The great majority of old people are in regular contact with their children, relatives or friends . . . where distance permits, the generations continue to shoulder their traditional obligations, of elders toward their children, and the children to the aged[33].

Throughout this chapter phrases such as 'the' family and 'dominant' family types have been used. These terms are misleading in so far as they could be interpreted to mean that all families fall into one or two categories or that social policies have consistently recognized one particular family structure, and services have been planned in some coherent fashion. Such is far from the facts. Evidence has been offered to show that at least three forms of family structure are believed to exist: extended, nuclear and modified extended family. Even these three are inadequate to describe the existing variant forms. Without debating the merits of one form over another, some analysis should be made on how existing policies affect these various forms and what assumptions of family structure underlie certain policy approaches.

For example, many policies are built on an implicit assumption that the extended family is the dominant structure and by definition this family is viewed as generally self-sufficient in meeting the needs of its members. The healthy family is one that does not seek support from extra-family institutions and for a family to do so is an admission that their support network is inadequate. When it breaks down the social welfare system intervenes on a residual basis. The State, for example, can take over certain functions or even completely substitute for the family when it is seen as incapable. Usually some sense of stigma is attached. Such was the official, explicit philosophy of the Poor Law era. Family members were held accountable by society through legal and social sanctions. While this has, to a large degree, been officially changed, it is still found in many policies. In some local authorities, for example, domiciliary services for the aged are withheld if the elderly person lives with or near an adult child. It is often immaterial whether the family is willing or capable to provide the necessary care. They are expected to do so and if they refuse the one who suffers is the elderly person. In fact, it could be hypothesized that in this period of economic strain, with little expansion in social welfare expenditures, this ideological approach will become more and more predominant. Eligibility will be tightened and families who are supporting their dependent members will receive few services. Increased demand will be met by developing more selective approaches to need, and risk and resources will be offered primarily to those handicapped individuals who either have no family or whose family are unwilling to care for them. Families who are willing to care will be expected to carry the total burden until they no longer can. If this were to occur, policies would effectively penalize the family.

This probable scenario is fairly representative of any number of dilemmas that face the State. Those influential in shaping policy or administering programmes may not want to 'penalize' the family but they also believe that the costs of providing services to them might result in fewer services for individuals who have no families. They further argue that priorities of need have to be established and the elderly who have families have relatively less need and must be assigned lower priority. The outcome of this decision will be that the family, in practice, serves the need of the State rather than the more commonly held belief that the State is the servant of its people.

Other policies clearly recognize the isolated nuclear family. As was shown earlier, existing housing policy with its emphasis on small houses and flats, makes it difficult for three-generational families to live together if they desire to do so. Even more telling is Young and Willmott's thesis that housing policy has made it extremely difficult for children to support their parents. While the generations might not want to live together, they do want to live in close proximity, and yet this is becoming less and less possible[34]. To some extent these two approaches, based on different assumptions about the family, are counterproductive. These policies set out to meet the physical housing needs of families but by and large ignored their social needs. Three-generational family units with a tradition of mutual support were disrupted and the elderly were forced to live at great distances from their children and grandchildren. The policies may have reached their stated objective of providing adequate housing to families but in doing so they had a negative impact on family life.

Finally, professionals and administrators have a tendency to define families in relation to the objectives of their specific organizations. For example, the public welfare system in the United States deals almost exclusively with female-headed families and its operational definition of a family is a 'broken' family. In practice this approach has been instrumental in breaking up the family by forcing the male member to desert. Single parent families there and in this country carry a stigma that relegates them to a less worthy category. The educational system focuses on the child and defines the family as a unit supportive to the educational system's objectives. Families are evaluated on the performance of their children. If the child does not do well, the family is held accountable and not the system. In the health services, especially those concerned with rehabilitation, professionals focus on the needs of the individual — the patient. In many cases rehabilitation personnel define the family in terms of the patient's needs. For example, home care programmes for the chronically ill and disabled define families as responsible or irresponsible depending on the availability and capacity of family members to assume the management of the patient. Family members are often viewed as necessary nuisances in the therapeutic process. An example of this is the strong bias against the father to be actively involved in the process of childbirth, despite a growing body of literature which suggests it has considerable value.

Policies and programmes are developed for specific individuals, the elderly, the handicapped, children, expectant mothers, mothers without husbands, the unemployed, persons who earn less than a certain income and so on. Services are provided to individuals on the implicit assumption that if an individual family member is provided with a service, the entire family will benefit. While most of our social policies do affect families, the nature of the impact is basically unknown, as the assumption has not been really tested. The United Kingdom, like most Western countries (France being an exception), does not have clearly stated policy on families. Family policy in this context is defined as a 'consensus on a core of family goals towards the realization of which the nation deliberately shapes programs and policy'[35]. Do existing policies recognize the family unit as a basic institution? Are families strengthened under most of these policies? Are individual policies complementary to each other or is it possible that they are contradictory or counterproductive? At this time it is impossible to answer these questions. They are rarely asked, or if raised are not treated in a comprehensive fashion. A meaningful treatment would require that all governmental policies be included in such an analysis: housing, income maintenance, tax, health, education and personal social services and attention to be given to both intra- and interdepartmental postures.

Summary

This chapter has discussed the theoretical role of the family as a social service in relation to the historical protective, socialization and caring functions of the family. While family structure has changed considerably over time, these functions appear to have survived, and in the opinion of some social scientists, to have been strengthed with the introduction of certain social welfare measures, most notably the provision of income maintenance for the dependent. In spite of earlier theoretical conclusions that the extended family has given way to the isolated nuclear family unit, considerable evidence has emerged over the past fifteen years that the nuclear family is not the dominant family type. On the contrary, while there are nuclear households, these households function in an extended family network characterized by a high degree of vertical and horizontal interaction and mutual support. The modern family household is nuclear, usually two generational, highly mobile, and consists more and more of two working spouses. These factors should deter families from carrying out certain caring functions for their dependent members, especially the frail elderly and the handicapped and yet there is some evidence to support the hypothesis that presentday families are both capable and willing to carry major responsibility.

 Social policies are built on some definition of the family and assumptions of the dominant form, whether extended, nuclear or a modification of each can either positively or negatively affect certain families. Policies can support the concept that the family has the primary responsibility for the care of their dependants and that only when they cannot or are unwilling to do so, will society intervene. Other policies can be viewed as instruments to take from the family some of these basic functions on the grounds that other institutions can do so more efficiently and effectively. Still another set of policies can be found that recognizes an informal family network sharing with and supported by the organized welfare system.

Litwak states the most obvious policy-relevant position. Beginning with the fact that a form of the extended family in fact exists, he suggests that neither the family nor the social welfare system specialize in one or more functions. Rather they share most functions because they 'bring together different but complementary means for achieving social goals'. He concludes:

In terms of the problem of maximizing available resources, the author would hypothesize that the modified family would be a more efficient unit than the nuclear family — all other things being equal. This results because the modified extended family, confronted with a problem, has a greater pool of resources to draw on than the nuclear family[36].

Maximizing available resources is, of course, the issue the country has to face. The State cannot conceivably afford to take over the total care of the dependant from the family. It does not have the resources, nor as some would argue the right to do so. Maximization requires a partnership, a sharing of the caring function, and the logical conclusion is the development of social policies that not only recognize but build on the recognition that a form of the extended family exists.

The next two chapters will focus on two groups, the elderly and the mentally handicapped child. Is there evidence of shared responsibility between the family and the social welfare system? What are the patterns of care? Are there trends that families are looking to the State to assume more and more responsibility for the caring function both in qualitative as well as quantitative terms? Is the State in practice supporting or substituting for the family? Finally, what do families with handicapped members actually want?

References

1. The concept of the family as a social service is somewhat ambiguous. Social services are usually defined as services designed to aid individuals and groups to meet basic needs, to enhance social functioning, to develop their potential, and to promote general wellbeing. The starting point in this chapter is that families are a social service in that they, as well as the community, society and the State, carry out these functions for family members. For a general discussion of what social services are see H. L. Wilensky and C. N. Lebeaux, *Industrial Society and Social Welfare*, New York, The Free Press, 1965, Ch. 6; M. Rein, *Social Policy: Issues of Choice and Change*, New York, Random House, 1970, Ch. 17; A. Kahn, *Social Policy and Social Services*, New York, Random House, 1973.

2. C. Zimmerman, *Family and Civilization*, New York, Harper, 1947.

3. M. Levy, jnr, *Modernization and the Structure of Societies*, Princeton University Press, 1966.

4. J. Folsom, *The Family and Democratic Society*, New York, Wiley, 1943.

5. This description of family functions and the sharing of these functions with other institutions draws on the following: C. Levi-Strauss, 'The family', in *Man, Culture, and Society*, ed., H. L. Shapiro, New York, Oxford University Press, 1956, pp. 261–85; R. MacIver and C. Page, *Society*, New York, Reinhart, 1949; T. Parsons, *The Social System*, Glencoe, Ill., The Free Press, 1951; F. Tönnies, *Community and Society — Gemeinschaft und Gesellschaft*, trans., C. P. Loomis, Michigan State University Press, 1957.

6. M. Sussman, 'Methodological problems in the study of the family', paper presented at the 81st Annual Convention of the American Psychological Association, 30 August 1973, Montreal.

7. E. Litwak, 'Extended kin relations in an industrial democratic society', *Social Structure and the Family: generational problems*, eds E. Shanas and G. Streib, Prentice-Hall, 1965, p. 290.

8. M. Sussman, 'Relationships of adult children with their parents in the United States', op. cit. (ref. 7), p. 66. Sussman traces the evolution of this idea from Durkheim, Weber, Tönnies, Simmel, Markheim, Linton, Wirth and Parsons.

9. P. Cox, 'Changes in ages at marriage, childbearing and death: preparation of estimates', in M. Young and P. Willmott, *The Symmetrical Family*, Routledge and Kegan Paul, 1973, Appendix 4, pp. 361–4.

10. R. Titmuss, 'The position of women', in *Essays on the Welfare State*, Unwin, 1958, p. 91.

11. M. Young and P. Willmott, op. cit. (ref. 9), p. 90.

12. H. Wilensky and C. Lebeaux, op. cit. (ref 7). Their full argument is that in the long run a low level of economic development is associated with a high fertility rate; high levels of economic development with high rates of growth lead to medium fertility rates; and high levels of economic development coupled with low rates of growth lead to low fertility rates.

13. Department of Employment, *Women and Work: A Statistical Survey*, Manpower Paper no. 9, HMSO, 1974, Table 8, p. 47.

14. For a discussion of why married women work see: V. Klein, *Britain's Married Women Workers*, Routledge and Kegan Paul, 1965; E. M. Harris, *Married Women in Industry*, London Institute of Personnel Management, 1954; A. Hunt, *A Survey of Women's Employment*, HMSO, 1968.

15. GSS, CSO, *Social Trends*, HMSO, 1974, p. 75.

16. See for example: J. Cresswell and P. Pasker, 'The frail who lead the frail', *New Society*, 5 May 1972; E. Shanas *et al.*, *Old People in Three Industrial Societies*, Routledge and Kegan Paul, 1968; P. Townsend, *Family Life of Old People*, Routledge and Kegan Paul, 1957.

17. OPCS, Social Survey Division, *The General Household Survey*, HMSO, 1973, pp. 149–51.

18. Sample Census, *Migration Tables*, Part 1, HMSO, 1966.

19. A. Harris, *Labour Mobility in Great Britain, 1953–63*, GSS, CSO, HMSO, 1967, p. 9.

20. A Harris, op. cit. (ref. 19), pp. 14–15; OPCS, op. cit. (ref. 17), p. 165.

21. M. Sussman. 'Relationships of adult children with their parents in the United States', op. cit. (ref. 7), p. 63.

22. See for example: M. Young and P. Willmott, *Family and Kinship in East London*, Routledge and Kegan Paul, 1957 and op. cit. (ref. 9); P. Townsend, op. cit. (ref. 16); J. Stehouwer, 'Relations between generations and the three-generation household in Denmark', op. cit. (ref. 7).

23. E. Litwak, op. cit. (ref. 7), p. 291.

24. M. Sussman, 'Relationships of adult children with their parents in the United States', op. cit. (ref. 7), pp. 63–4; M. Young and P. Willmott, op. cit. (ref. 9), pp. 266–7 make the same point.

25. OPCS, Census, 1971, *Age, Marital Condition and General Tables*, General Register Office, 1974, Table 5.

26. M. Anderson, *Family Structure in Nineteenth-Century Lancashire*, Cambridge University Press, 1971, p. 178.

27. M. Rosenheim, 'Social welfare and its implications for family living', op. cit. (ref. 7), p. 213.

28. *Report of the Royal Commission on the Poor Laws and Relief of Distress.* Cd 4499, 1909, Vol. 3, p. 259.

29. E. Shanas, 'The unmarried old person in the United States: living arrangements and care in illness, myth or fact', paper prepared for the International Social Service Research Seminar in Gerontology, Markaryd, Sweden, August 1963.

30. This is the basic conclusion drawn from data collected in three countries: the United Kingdom, Denmark and the United States. See E. Shanas *et al.*, op. cit. (ref. 16), Ch. 7.

31. See for example: E. Shanas *et al.*, op. cit. (ref. 16); P. Townsend, op. cit. (ref. 16); M. Young and P. Willmott, op. cit. (ref. 22); A. Schorr, *Filial Responsibility in the Modern American Family*, US Dept of Health, Education and Welfare, Washington D.C., 1960; M. Sussman and L. Burchinall, 'Parental aid to married children: implications for family functioning', *Marriage and Family Living*, **24**, Nov. 1962, 320–32.

32. Age Concern, *Attitudes of the Retired and the Elderly*, 1974.

33. World Health Organization, *Mental Health Problems of the Ageing and the Aged*, Technical Report Series, no. 171, Geneva, 1959.

34. M. Young and P. Willmott, op. cit. (ref. 22).

35. A. Schorr, 'Family policy in the United States', in *Explorations in Social Policy*, New York, Basic Books, 1968, p. 143.

36. E. Litwak, op. cit. (ref. 7), p. 309.

3 The family and the elderly

While the general concern of this study is the relationship between the family and the social welfare system in the care of the socially dependent, two distinct sub-groups have been identified as meriting special attention. A number of reasons were identified in Chapter 1 to justify their inclusion: the numbers involved, their needs, and the scale of resources currently allocated. Both groups are heavy consumers of social welfare services, a pattern that is expected to continue over the next thirty years. A second set of reasons is related to the particular nature of the dependency and the pressures on families with elderly or mentally handicapped members. The ageing process and most forms of severe mental retardation are irreversible. The old cannot become young again and the mentally handicapped child is not likely to be cured. Granted that appropriate rehabilitation and social care can result in sufficient improvements in functional status. Neither condition is static and wide variation in capacity can be found. Finally, it was hypothesized that if there are shifts in the relationship between the family and the State with the latter assuming more responsibility, this increased transfer initially might be perceived with these groups of dependants since both the elderly and mentally handicapped tend to be regarded as 'worthy' dependants (in a relative sense) with less stigma associated with these conditions. The word 'relative' is important here. It has been thirty years since the passage of key legislation for the elderly and fifteen years since the status of the mentally handicapped began to change. Other groups, for example, the single parent family, the alcoholic and drug addict, or the family in which a child is abused, still carry a strong stigma.

This chapter focuses specifically on the elderly and analyses changes in the elderly population that have occurred in this century, their physical and social characteristics, and patterns of social welfare provision. While many of the demographic shifts have been reported extensively elsewhere, it is useful to highlight in summary form those that are crucial for social policy, with emphasis on projections over the next thirty years.

Since 1901 the elderly population has increased at a rate far in excess of the growth in the general population, a trend that is expected to continue throughout this century. Overall, the rate of increase was greater over the first fifty years with relatively less growth over the second half. However, this latter period will be characterized by significant increases in the older elderly groups, especially those over eighty-four years of age.

While this reflects medical, environmental and social advances and to some degree might be viewed as an indicator of overall improvement in standards of living in a developed nation, it has brought with it the need to develop a new social infrastructure to maintain the quality of life (a phrase much abused and almost meaningless in practical terms) of these persons.

Table 3.1   Per cent increase in the elderly population, 1901–2001, England and Wales

Population	1901–51	1951–2001	1901–2001
Total population	34	27	70
Population 65 and over	215	50	372
Population 75 and over	245	82	530
Population 85 and over	294	233	1,212

Sources: GSS, CSO, Annual Abstract of Statistics, HMSO, no. 109, 1972, pp. 9, 16; OPCS, Census, 1971, Great Britain, Age, Marital Condition and General Tables, HMSO, 1974.

Reductions in mortality and increased longevity are inevitably accompanied by higher rates of morbidity, chronic illness and disability. Thus social welfare mechanisms over time have come to include policies on income maintenance, housing and residential care, specialized medical care and various social support services.

That the State has made a commitment to the elderly is indisputable. Since 1963 almost one-half of key social welfare expenditures have been allocated to this group, respresenting only 16 per cent of the population[1]. The word 'commitment' is used despite the fact that a number of surveys have shown considerable shortfalls in some of the services required by the elderly[2], and that these shortfalls are cited by others as evidence of lack of real commitment by the State[3].

Table 3.2   Social welfare expenditure on the elderly – percentages

Service	1963/64	% GNP	1971/72	% GNP
Social security	62.0	4.1	60.0	5.4
Health and welfare	27.0	1.1	28.0	1.5
Combined social security health and welfare	49.0	5.2	48.0	6.9
Per capita expenditure on elderly	£188		£237	

Note: Per capita expenditures at 1963/64 prices.

Source: D. Wroe, 'The elderly', Social Trends, GSS, CSO, HMSO, no. 4, 1973, 23–33.

In 1971/72, almost 7 per cent of the gross national product (GNP) representing 14 per cent of all public expenditure was consumed by the elderly through various income maintenance and health and welfare services[4]. The State is now faced with a number of perplexing policy questions. Can this level of expenditure be maintained over the next thirty years? Can the projected increase of an additional million elderly, the majority of whom will be very old, be dealt with? If the increased numbers require inevitable increases in social welfare expenditures, will this have an effect on the State's ability to reduce the recognized shortfalls between current and desirable levels of service provision? What portion of the GNP or public expenditure would be necessary and where would these resources come from? If economic growth slows down and if total available social welfare resources shrink, would increases for the elderly be made at the expense of other population groups? The issue of shared responsibility between the family and the State has become and will continue to be a critical policy question.

Characteristics of the elderly

At the turn of the century, the elderly numbered slightly over 1.5 million people, about 5 per cent of the total population. Less than three of every ten elderly were seventy-five years of age or older and approximately 50,000 people were aged eighty-five years or more, or three of every one hundred elderly. Over the following thirty years (1901—31) the elderly population doubled, but the age structure of the elderly remained the same. Over seven of every ten elderly were in the age group sixty-five to seventy-four years of age. Since 1951, there have been significant shifts in these ratios. By 1961, 36 per cent of the elderly were seventy-five years of age or more, by 1981 they will represent 38 per cent and at the turn of the century, 44 per cent.

Table 3.3   *Elderly population as percentage of total population, England and Wales*

Year	Total pop. ('000s)	Per cent over 65	Per cent elderly over 75	Per cent elderly over 85
1901	32,528	4.7	25.9	3.3
1911	36,070	5.2	24.3	3.4
1921	37,887	6.0	25.1	3.3
1931	39,952	7.4	24.6	3.2
1951	43,758	11.0	28.4	4.1
1961	46,105	11.9	30.5	5.5
1971	48,750	13.3	28.6	6.6
1981	50,817	14.3	31.6	6.4
1991	53,025	14.0	33.6	8.0
2001	55,473	13.0	34.6	9.1

Source: GSS, CSO, *Annual Abstract of Statistics*, HMSO, no. 109, 1972, p. 16.

In real terms, this means that in thirty years' time there will be 2.5 million people over seventy-four (an absolute increase of 641,000 over 1971) and 656,000 people over eighty-four (an increase of almost 250,000). Thus the State is faced with the prospect of not only planning for more elderly persons, but also given these shifts in the age structure, for significant increases in the number of the very old and the frail elderly, and it is this group who have historically been the heavy consumers of the social welfare services.

Another facet of these demographic shifts worth noting is the sex composition of the elderly population. In 1851, 55 per cent of all elderly were female and by 1901 they represented 57 per cent. Over the next thirty years it appears that the ratio will stabilize at 61 per cent. It is also clear that not only will there be more elderly women, but they are more likely to be older than elderly men. The more significant differences are found in the group eighty-five years of age and older. Over a period of fifty years (1951–2001), the percentage of men in this age group will have increased from 3.1 to 5.5 per cent, while for women the figures are 4.8 per cent and a startling 11.4 per cent. By the year 2001, not only will there be 656,000 people aged eighty-five and over, but three of every four will be women, or close to 500,000.

Table 3.4 *Age and sex distribution of the elderly population, 1951–2001, England and Wales*

	1951	1961	1971	1981	1991	2001
Males						
65–74	69.5	67.4	70.5	68.7	65.3	63.7
75–84	27.4	28.3	25.1	27.5	29.8	30.8
over 84	3.1	4.3	4.4	3.8	4.9	5.5
	(100.0)	(100.0)	(100.0)	(100.0)	(100.0)	(100.0)
Females						
65–74	66.2	61.9	60.5	57.8	54.0	51.4
75–84	29.0	31.8	31.6	34.2	36.0	37.2
over 84	4.8	6.3	7.9	8.0	10.0	11.4
	(100.0)	(100.0)	(100.0)	(100.0)	(100.0)	(100.0)
Per cent male	40.9	38.2	38.4	38.8	38.8	39.1
Per cent female	59.1	61.8	61.6	61.2	61.2	60.9
	(100.0)	(100.0)	(100.0)	(100.0)	(100.0)	(100.0)

Source: GSS, CSO, *Annual Abstract of Statistics*, HMSO, no. 109, 1972, p. 16.

Since 1851 there has been a consistent shift in the marital status of the elderly. Men are more likely to be married than their counterparts of the nineteenth century. Among younger elderly men (the age group sixty-five to seventy-four), eight of every ten were married in 1971, compared to six in 1851. The same trend is found in the older age group (men over seventy-four years of age), four in ten were married in 1851 compared to six in ten in 1971. This pattern is also found among younger elderly women. The major exception is found among elderly women over seventy-four years of age. Two of every three were either widowed or divorced in both 1851 and 1971.

Table 3.5   *Marital status of the elderly 1901—2001, England and Wales*

Status	1901		1951		1971		2001	
	65—74	75 and over	65—74	75 and over	65—74	75 and over	65—74	75 and over
Males								
Married	63.1	42.6	72.2	50.0	78.5	57.3	1,415	592
Single	7.8	6.5	8.9	8.2	8.0	6.9	129	62
Wid./Div.	29.1	50.8	18.9	41.8	13.5	35.8	247	368
Females								
Married	36.8	16.2	42.2	19.8	45.4	18.5	1,026	397
Single	11.2	11.1	16.1	17.0	14.3	16.1	304	327
Wid./Div.	52.0	72.7	41.7	63.2	40.3	65.4	920	1,402

Note: The figures for 1901—71 are expressed as percentages. The figures for 2001 are estimated numbers ('000s) for each category and are based on 1970 patterns. While these estimates are tenuous, they are included to show what the situation might be at that time.

Sources: GCS, CSO, *Annual Abstract of Statistics*, HMSO, no. 109, 1972, p. 26; OPCS, Census, 1971, Great Britain, *Age, Marital Conditions and General Tables*, HMSO, 1974; GSS, CSO, *Social Trends*, no. 9, HMSO, 1974, Table 26, p. 90.

More striking are the differences in marital status between men and women. In 1901, twice as many men as women in the age group sixty-five to seventy-four were married, and two-and-a-half times as many in the older group. By 1971 the differences in the younger group had shrunk slightly, but among those seventy-five years and over, men were three times more likely to be married than women. Three of every five men were married compared to one of every five women. If these ratios were to remain constant, by the year 2001 there will be almost 1.75 million women over the age of seventy-four without a spouse (single, widowed and divorced). When the unmarried men are added, the number exceeds 2 million people.

This brief analysis has highlighted a number of changes that have taken place over the past seventy years, trends that are likely to continue for the rest of the century. In 1901 those over sixty-four years of age represented slightly under 5 per cent of the total population. By 1971 the elderly constituted 13 per cent, an increase in absolute numbers of 5 million. This shift has been accompanied by a significant growth of the very old, those eighty-five years of age and over.

Approximately six of every ten elderly are female. Females not only make up more of the elderly population but they are likely to be older than elderly males. While more of the elderly are married than previously, two of every three women over seventy-four years and nine of every ten over eighty-four years were widowed or divorced in 1971.

If current population projections hold over the next thirty years, by 2001 there will be an additional 727,000 elderly (the peak year will actually be 1991 with an increase of almost 1 million elderly over 1971), of whom 88 per cent will be over age seventy-four and 41 per cent over age eighty-four. Of this latter group, the aged elderly, most will be widowed or divorced women.

Functional status of the elderly

While it is generally agreed that the elderly are more likely to be disabled and have higher rates of handicapping conditions than the general population, it is difficult to locate comparable time series data to observe relevant historical patterns. Most studies dealing with the aged are not national in scope but area specific, and the sampling procedures used limit broader application of the findings[5]. Over the past fifteen years there have been three national surveys, the first in 1962, the second in 1968, and the last in 1971[6]. However, it is impossible to correlate the findings of even these due to definitional differences.

The 1962 Survey used a scale developed by Townsend and attempted to measure an individual's ability to perform minimal personal care tasks. It is similar to other 'activity of daily living' (ADL) scales and is concerned with mobility and personal care. Respondents were asked whether they could perform six basic tasks and then scored on a composite index ranging from nought to twelve. A zero rating indicated independent status while a score of seven or more indicated that 'the individual can do all six tasks only with difficulty and at least one task not at all, or that he can do some of these tasks with difficulty, and some not at all'[7].

The 1968 Survey attempted to measure levels of impairment, disability and handicapping conditions. Impairment was defined as 'lacking part or all of a limb or having a defective limb; or having a defective organ or mechanism of the body which stops or limits getting about, work or self care'. Disablement is 'the loss or reduction of functional ability' and handicap is 'the disadvantage or restriction of activity caused by disability'[8]. Unlike the 1962 Survey, where respondents were asked whether they could do something, individuals were actually tested as to their capacity.

The 1971 Survey set out to measure the prevalence of limitation of activity caused by long-standing chronic sickness. Chronic sickness was defined as 'a long-standing illness, disability or infirmity which limits a persons' overall activity level'[9]. As in the 1962 Survey, respondents were asked about their functional ability and not tested. Table 3.6 shows the difficulty in relating these findings.

Table 3.6   *Prevalence of incapacity, impairment and limitations among the elderly: three surveys*

Age group	1962 Survey			1968 Survey			1971 Survey	
	None	Some incap.	7 or more	None	Im- paired	Severely handi- capped	None	With limita- tions
65–74	63.8	36.2	2.7	77.9	22.1	0.8	58.8	41.2
75 and over	38.3	61.7	11.0	62.2	37.8	4.4	51.7	48.3
Total 65 and over	54.9	45.1	6.0	73.4	26.6	1.8	56.5	43.5

Sources: Adapted from: E. Shanas *et al.*, *Old People in Three Industrial Societies*, Routledge and Kegan Paul, 1968, Table 2.10, p. 36 (1962 Survey).
OPCS, Social Survey Division, A. Harris, *Handicapped and Impaired in Great Britain*, HMSO, 1971, Table 2, p. 5 and Table 9, p. 18 (1968 Survey).
OPCS, Social Survey Division, *The General Household Survey*, HMSO, 1973, Table 8.2, p. 267 (1971 Survey).

The two surveys of perceived or subjective incapacity, ten years apart, show both complementary and contradictory elements. Both studies show that between 55 and 56 per cent of the elderly population have no limitations. However, the similarities end there. The 1962 Survey found that only 38 per cent of the elderly (seventy-five years of age and older) had no limitations, while the 1971 Survey estimated that 52 per cent in this age group were not incapacitated. Both surveys differ significantly from the 1968 study. Harris found that over seven of every ten elderly suffered no 'impairment' — a category that appears to approximate 'incapacity' and 'limitations' as used by the others. One explanation might be the fact that the Harris survey tested ability while the others asked the respondents whether they were able to carry out certain functions. Another possible factor is that the Harris study appears to have defined impairment and dependency more strictly.

Both the 1962 and 1968 Surveys provide information on the more severely affected. The former defined 'severe incapacity' on the basis of an individual scoring seven or more on the composite scale: 6 per cent of the elderly were located in this group. The 1968 Survey found slightly less than 2 per cent of the elderly to be severely handicapped (Categories 1–5). If the 'appreciably handicapped' (Category 6) were added to this group, the percentage would still only be increased to 3.7 per cent. All three surveys show that the prevalence of incapacity or handicapping conditions increases with age and the two studies that identify severe incapacity suggest that the elderly over seventy-four years of age are three to four times more likely to be classified as such than those aged sixty-five to seventy-four.

Since the Harris survey employed a stricter set of definitions than the other two studies and also because her focus was specifically on ascertaining the prevalence of handicapping conditions, this analysis has used her rates to estimate the future at risk population. Based on her findings, in 1971 there were an estimated 1,700,000 impaired elderly in England and Wales. Two of every three were female and half were over seventy-four years of age[10]. Over 700,000 elderly were classified as handicapped (116,000 very severely handicapped; 215,000 severely handicapped; and 380,000 appreciably handicapped). Over 72 per cent of all elderly handicapped were women and 52 per cent were over seventy-four years. Table 3.7 presents estimates of the number of the very severely handicapped over the next thirty years. They are straight line projections based on the age specific prevalence rates for men and women applied to existing population projections.

By the year 2001 the number of the very severely handicapped elderly will have increased by 25 per cent or an additional 30,000 people. One

Table 3.7 *Number of very severely handicapped elderly, 1971—2001, England and Wales ('000s)*

Sex and age groups	1971	1981	1991	2001
Male				
65—74	14.2	15.6	15.2	14.5
75 and over	21.5	25.7	29.3	29.8
Total	35.7	41.3	44.5	44.3
Female				
65—74	21.0	22.3	21.4	19.5
75 and over	59.7	70.7	79.0	80.1
Total	80.7	93.0	100.4	99.6
Totals				
65—74	35.2	37.9	36.6	34.0
75 and over	81.2	96.4	108.3	109.9
Total	116.4	134.3	144.9	143.9

Note: 'Very severely handicapped' includes only those in Categories 1—3 (p. 13).

Source: Projections based on A. Harris, *Handicapped and Impaired in Great Britain*, OPCS, Social Survey Division, HMSO, 1971, pp. 5, 18.

hundred thousand of the very severely handicapped will be women, 80,000 of whom will be over seventy-four years of age. Harris further estimated that 38 per cent of the very severely handicapped were either bedfast or chairfast; 75 per cent of these are women and the majority are over seventy-four[11]. This means that if the same factors hold, in twenty years' time there will be over 55,000 immobile elderly persons, over 41,000 of whom will be elderly women over the age of seventy-four and 80 per cent of whom will be widowed, divorced or single (Table 3.5).

Living status of the elderly

Since 1911 less than 1.4 per cent of the total population have been residents in institutions at the time of the decennial census. The data for 1971 actually show a slight reduction in percentage in institutions over the previous twenty years. While the rate of institutionalization for the elderly has been two to three times higher than the general population, with the exception of 1911, the percentage of institutionalized elderly has consistently been under 5 per cent. This figure includes both long- and short-term stays. In 1961 Shanas estimated that of the total elderly institutional population, 80 per cent (3.6 per cent) could be classified as long-stay residents[12]. Historically, then, 95 per cent or more of the elderly have been living in non-institutional settings.

Table 3.8   *Residential status of elderly, 1911–71, England and Wales*

	1911	1931	1951	1961	1971
Population ('000s)	36,070	39,952	43,758	46,105	48,750
Per cent in institutions	1.25	1.34	1.37	1.37	1.32
Elderly ('000s)	1,876	2,956	4,813	5,486	6,484
Per cent in institutions	5.3	3.5	3.5	4.5	4.7

Note: Institutional residence: 1911: workhouses, lunatic asylums, prisons, hospitals for the sick; 1931: Poor Law institutions; homes for the insane; hospitals and nursing homes; prisons, reformatories and other places of detention; homes for cripples, the blind, the deaf and dumb; 1951: hospitals and nursing homes; institutions for the mentally ill and mentally deficient; homes for the aged and infirm, reformatories and other places for detention; childrens' homes and hostels, homes for the blind, deaf and dumb and cripples; 1961–71: psychiatric hospitals; all other institutions; homes for old and disabled persons; homes for children; places of detention.

Sources: General Register Office, *Censuses, 1911, 1931, 1951, 1961, 1971*, HMSO.

Living status of the non-institutionalized elderly population   In 1971, 26 per cent of the elderly were living alone[13], a slight increase from 1965 when the corresponding figure was 25 per cent[14]. Women are more likely to live alone showing the strong correlation between living status and age and marital status; 32 per cent of all elderly women lived alone compared to 13 per cent of elderly men; 55 per cent of elderly men lived with their wives compared to 33 per cent of the elderly women. Most significant to the focus of this study is the fact that in 1971 one of every four elderly persons, comprising over 1 million people, lived with their children in extended family households.

Table 3.9   *Living status of non-institutional elderly, 1971, Great Britain*

Sex and age group	Alone (%)	With spouse (%)	Children only (%)	Spouse/ children (%)	Others (%)
Males					
65–74	11.3	58.3	2.6	15.6	12.2
75 and over	19.1	46.9	6.0	12.1	15.9
Females					
65–74	27.9	39.4	7.0	11.2	14.5
75 and over	42.3	15.6	11.5	8.8	21.8
Total	26.0	39.9	6.7	11.8	15.7

Source: Adapted from GSS, CSO, *Social Trends*, HMSO, 1974, p. 91.

While the 1962 National Survey documented the amount of family care provided to the elderly, unfortunately no similar studies have been undertaken since then. In 1962, however, families appeared to have provided a significant amount of care. Shanas reported that over 80 per cent of all elderly in the United Kingdom either lived in the same household with their children or less than half an hour's journey from them. While proximity does not mean that they will have frequent contact, it is a predisposing factor. In fact, 69 per cent of the elderly reported that they saw at least one of their children on the day of the interview or the preceding day, and 86 per cent within the previous week. Six of every ten old persons received help from their children on a regular basis[15].

Of the elderly who were unable to do their own housework, bath themselves, or prepare meals, over one-third were assisted by their children, and if all relatives are included the percentage is increased to over 40 per cent. Relatively few were receiving help from the formal social welfare system (excluding income maintenance and medical care)[16].

Harris's survey of the non-institutionalized handicapped and impaired, carried out six years later would suggest that this pattern had not changed. The 1968 study estimated that 33 per cent of those who could not manage their housekeeping functions were helped primarily by their children, 10 per cent by their siblings, 5 per cent by other relatives and 6 per cent by friends or neighbours[17]. Another indicator of the extent of family

Table 3.10　Percentage of elderly who received help from families

	Housework*	Heavy housework	Bathing	Meals
Spouse	31	18	15	39
Child in household	22	25	28	30
Child outside household	13	11	5	4
Others in household	9	7	6	11
Others outside household	13	11	5	6
Privately paid domestic help	—	11	0	0
Social services	4	9	7	4
None	7	13	37	11
Per cent of sample unable to do task or having difficulty	30	49	7	11

* Applies only to people ill in bed.

Note: Percentages relate only to those elderly who were assessed as needing assistance in carrying out these functions.

Source: Adapted from E. Shanas *et al.*, *Old People in Three Industrial Societies*, Routledge and Kegan Paul, 1968, pp. 113–20.

support for the elderly is the living arrangements of the handicapped elderly. Whereas 19 per cent of all elderly lived with their children, 36 per cent of the handicapped elderly did so; only 21 per cent of the elderly handicapped lived alone, compared with 26 per cent of all elderly. Living status was also correlated with the severity of the handicapping condition. One-half of the very severely handicapped lived with children, 5 per cent lived alone. It should also be remembered that 72 per cent of the handicapped are women and seven of ten were over seventy-five years of age.

Table 3.11　*Living status of non-institutionalized elderly handicapped, England and Wales*

	Alone (%)	With spouse (%)	Children only (%)	Spouse/ children (%)	Others (%)	1971 total ('000s)
Very severe	5.2	29.3	32.9	16.5	16.1	116
Severe	23.7	32.2	16.9	17.9	9.3	215
Appreciable	23.6	31.8	15.6	18.3	10.6	380
Total	21.0	31.6	18.5	18.0	10.9	711

Source: Adapted from A. Harris, *Handicapped and Impaired in Great Britain*, OPCS, Social Survey Division, HMSO, 1971, p. 24.

To appreciate the pressures these frail elderly bring to their families it is useful to go back to the definitions used in the survey[18]. One hundred and sixteen thousand elderly were classified as 'very severely handicapped'. This group was defined as those who were

- mentally impaired or senile, unable to understand questions or give rational answers;
- permanently bedfast;
- confined to a chair, unable to get in and out without the aid of a person;
- unable to feed themselves or need someone to assist using the WC;
- doubly incontinent or could not be left alone since they might harm themselves.

The severely handicapped (215,000) included those who

- experienced difficulty doing everything or found most things difficult and some impossible;
- found most things difficult or three or four items difficult and some impossible.

The appreciably handicapped number 380,000 elderly who can do a fair amount for themselves but have difficulty with some items and require some assistance. An estimated 261,000 handicapped elderly (57,000 very severely handicapped, 75,000 severely handicapped and 129,000 appreciably handicapped) are living with their children.

The severity of these pressures on families has been well documented. Sainsbury and Grad report on the considerable burden born by the geriatric patient's family, preceding their referral to a community mental health service[19]. Eighty per cent of families who sought help were facing problems, 40 per cent severe problems; two-thirds of the elderly patients needed nursing care and one-half of these needed it constantly; 44 per cent of the elderly family members were demanding excessive attention and companionship.

In half of the families the social life of the family members was restricted and in six of every ten families the physical wellbeing of the relative who assumed the caring responsibility of the elderly person was affected. Family income was reduced by at least 10 per cent in a number of cases, and in 36 per cent of the sample, the domestic routine of the home was upset. Given these strains on the total family, the authors found it 'remarkable that more than one-third of the families had endured this situation for more than two years before contacting a psychiatrist'. Apparently these families were prepared to cope, even at considerable costs to themselves.

Lowther and Williamson in a survey of old people discharged from a geriatric unit found that only 1.2 per cent of their relatives unreasonably refused to provide home care. In fact, relatives were five times more likely to provide care to the severely disabled patients willingly[20]. Cresswell and Pasker, in examining this issue strongly charged that society is 'currently exploiting the heroism and willingness to put up with hardship, of a very large number of old people' in so far as few had actually requested help, or when sought, received a minimal level of service[21].

Given these increases in the numbers of elderly persons, particularly the frail elderly, and the nature of the demands they make on their families, how has the social welfare system evolved to provide needed care? Has the State increasingly taken over the caring function as some believe or is it 'exploiting' the family? Has State involvement resulted in an increased transfer of responsibility from the family? Do social policies substitute for the family, or do they support the family through some sharing of the caring function? The next section examines patterns of institutional care — the extreme form of transfer. Have there been increases in rates of institutionalization and what trends might be anticipated over the next few decades?

This issue of 'exploitation' is discussed in Chapter 6. It is an emotionally charged phrase and requires some elaboration. The evidence, however, is clear. Families have and are providing levels of social care to elderly parents or relatives that involve physical, emotional, social and economic costs.

The institutional population   While the vast majority of the elderly are living in non-institutional settings, it is necessary to examine patterns of institutionalization to see whether they show any trends. As discussed earlier (see Table 3.8) the percentage of institutionalized elderly (both long- and short-term stays) was lowest during the decades 1931 to 1951 (3.5 per cent). The decade 1951—61 saw a sharp increase to 4.5 per cent, levelling off at 4.7 per cent in 1971. This section will focus on two types of institutional settings, residential care facilities and mental hospitals, since it is here that most of the long-term elderly are to be found.

At the turn of the century a little more than 90,000 elderly persons sixty-five years of age and over were residents in various Poor Law institutions (most of these were workhouses). Indoor relief appeared to have become the dominant form of social care for the elderly over the second half of the nineteenth century. From 1871 to 1905 the institutional population had increased by 35 per cent while the numbers receiving 'outdoor relief' increased by only 17 per cent. Over one-half of the elderly in these institutions were males. By 1911 both the absolute numbers and the percentage of elderly had begun to decline giving support to the arguments of Anderson[22] and Rosenheim[23] that with the development of income maintenance programmes (old age pensions) many families found it possible to support their aged parents in the community.

Since 1952 the number of elderly in residential care provided by or on behalf of local government has increased by 69,000 or 160 per cent. When the number in various private facilities are added to this the increase is over 80,000. Two points must be emphasized, The first is that the State, following the Second World War, has made considerable expenditures in this form of social care when it decided to do away with the large Poor

Table 3.12 *Trends in residential care, 1906—73, England and Wales ('000s)*

Year	Eld. as per cent of pop.	Eld. in care prov. by or for local authorities	Elderly in other res. care facilities	Total elderly in res. care	Per cent elderly in res. care
1906	4.7 (1901)	90	—	90	5.60
1911	5.3	82	—	82	4.37
1921		61	—	61	2.68
1931		60	—	60	2.03
1952	11.0 (1951)	43	16	59	1.19
1954		49	17	66	1.29
1955		51	18	69	1.32
1956		57	20	77	1.44
1959		71	24	85	1.77
1961	11.9	76	24	100	1.82
1964		86	24	110	1.89
1965		90	25	115	1.96
1966	12.4	92	26	118	2.01
1967		95	27	122	2.01
1968		99	28	127	2.06
1969		102	29	131	2.10
1970	13.3 (1971)	105	29	134	2.12
1972		109	29	138	2.09
1973		112	29	141	2.07

Sources: 1906: *Report of the Royal Commission on the Poor Laws,* Cd 4499, London, HMSO, 1909. Figures are for Poor Law institutions.
1911—31: Figures are taken from Decennial Census for appropriate decades and refer to various Poor Law institutions.
1952—73: Figures are derived from Annual Reports of the Ministry of Health, later the Department of Health and Social Security.

Law institutions as the primary form of care for the elderly. In doing so it provided for the first time a viable alternative for many of the elderly and their families. The second point is that despite the fact that residential care rates increased over the past thirty years, current rates are still three times less than those at the turn of the century. Since the mid-1960s the percentage of elderly in residential care facilities appears to have stabilized at 2.1 per cent.

These figures are somewhat misleading on face value. Many of the elderly in the first half of the century were still in institutions that had been reclassified as chronic hospitals or mental illness hospitals. While it is impossible to identify the number of elderly who resided in all these institutions on a more or less permanent basis, statistics are available on patients in mental hospitals. On the whole these stays were long-term and if these data are included, the revised table would be:

Table 3.13   *Trends in long-term residential care, 1911–73, England and Wales ('000s)*

Year	Total elderly in res. care	Elderly in mental hosp.	Total	Per cent elderly in institutions
1911	82	15	97	5.17
1921	61	16	77	3.39
1931	60	26	86	2.91
1952	59	45	104	2.10
1954	66	46	112	2.16
1955	69	47	116	2.21
1956	77	48	125	2.35
1959	95	50	145	2.69
1961	100	52	152	2.77
1964	110	52	162	2.79
1965	115	53	168	2.85
1966	118	53	171	2.92
1967	122	54	176	2.89
1968	127	54	181	2.95
1969	131	55	186	2.97
1970	134	55	189	2.98
1972	138	56	194	2.94
1973	141	56	197	2.88

Sources: Figures for elderly patients in mental hospitals are taken from appropriate Decennial Census reports. Estimates have been made for the interdecennial years from various annual reports of the Ministry of Health, later the Department of Health and Social Security.

Between 1952 and 1973 the long-term institutional population almost doubled in size, representing an increase from 2 to 3 per cent of the total elderly population. This is still significantly less than the percentage institutionalized at the turn of the century. To show the magnitude of the difference, if the earlier rates of institutionalizations were applied to the 1973 population, instead of 197,000 elderly in long-term institutional care, the figures would have been 380,000 (1906 rate), 354,000 (1911 rate) and 232,000 (1921 rate).

Still, the rate of institutionalization has increased since 1952, giving an excess of 55,000 to 65,000 elderly over the last five years (applying the 1952 rate). Before attributing this excess to greater demand and an indication of increased transfer from families to the State, it is necessary to distinguish the differences in the age structure of the elderly population.

In the late 1950s the residential care rates for the elderly were lower than the rates in 1971, 17 per 1,000 elderly compared with 21 per 1,000.

Table 3.14 *Residential care rates per 1,000 elderly 1958—59 and 1971, England and Wales*

	1958—59	1971
Males		
65—69	5	4
70—74	12	9
75—79	23	19
80—84	48	42
Over 84	63	88
Females		
65—69	3	4
70—74	9	10
75—79	19	23
80—84	41	55
Over 84	79	122
Total	17	21

Sources: 1958—59: P. Townsend, 'The effects of family structure on the likelihood of admission to an institution in old age: the application of a general theory', in *Social Structure and the Family: Generational Relations*, eds E. Shanas and G. Streib, Prentice-Hall, 1965, p. 169.
1971: OPCS, Census, 1971, *Non-Private Households*, HMSO, 1974.

However, it is clear that the increase is in great part due to the fact that the elderly population itself changed. Between these two periods, the residential care rates for males between sixty-five and eighty years of age actually decreased, while the rates for women remained basically the same. It is in the older group that the shift has occurred, those of eighty-five years and older, and especially among females. Over the past five years, four of every ten residents were eighty-five or older and eight of every ten were over seventy-four or older. From 1951 to 1971 the total elderly population increased by 35 per cent, the elderly population over seventy-four years by 36 per cent, and those over eighty-four by 117 per cent. Between 25 per cent and 33 per cent of all new admissions or applications for admission were over eighty-four years and the great majority have been single, widowed, or divorced[24].

Four studies, spanning fifteen years, have identified the same set of reasons why people seek admission to residential care[25]. The major reason noted is that the elderly (by and large the frail elderly) are unable to look after themselves or anticipate that they will not be able to in the near future. Admission is often preceded by an illness or death of the family member who provided care for the elderly person. Loneliness was the precipitating factor is only 7 to 8 per cent of the admissions, while difficulties with relatives accounted for less than 10 per cent. The pattern that emerges, then, does not appear to support the charge that families are giving up the caring function. Before discussing the community support systems for the elderly and their families, a series of projections can be made related to institutional care.

Table 3.15   *Projections of institutional elderly population, England and Wales ('000s)*

	1971	*1981*	*1991*	*2001*
Residential care				
65 and over	133	150	153	148
75 and over	88	109	118	118
85 and over	48	53	67	74
Mental hospitals				
65 and over	56	62	64	62
75 and over	21	26	29	29
85 and over	7	7	10	11
Total long-term institutional population				
65 and over	189	212	217	210
75 and over	109	135	147	147
85 and over	55	60	77	85

Note: Projection of institutional population based on age-specific rates for 1971. Residential care: 65 and over — 20.6 per 1,000 over 64; 75 and over — 47.5 per 1,000 over 74; 85 and over — 113.1 per 1,000 over 84. Mental hospitals: 65 and over — 8.6 per 1,000 over 64; 75 and over — 11.5 per 1,000 over 74; 85 and over — 16.2 per 1,000 over 84.

Source: Population projections taken from GSS, CSO, *Annual Abstract of Statistics*, HMSO, no. 9, 1972, p. 16.

These projections are based on current rates of institutionalization and assume that few changes will be made in social policy, and the same demand patterns will continue. If these assumptions hold, an overall increase of 11 per cent among the institutionalized elderly over the next thirty years can be expected. However, the increase among the institutional population over seventy-four years will be 35 per cent and for those over eighty-four, 54 per cent. In 1971 the age structure of the elderly residential care population was 66 per cent over seventy-four and 36 per cent over eighty-four. Corresponding figures for the year 2001 will be 80 and 50 per cent.

Because these projections are based on current rates of utilization, they are offered as not only conservative estimates, but as the bare minimum of places required to maintain current levels. They anticipate the changes in the age structure of the elderly population but do not allow for shifts in policy nor changing patterns of family care. In fact, they assume families will continue to provide care at the present rate.

Even if eight of every ten residents in these institutions were to be over seventy-four, and half were over eighty-four, and further, if all of these were very severely handicapped elderly (which is unlikely), these figures would account for only 75 per cent of this at-risk group. Finally, these projections estimate that the total elderly in residential care facilities and mental hospitals will peak at 3 per cent of the elderly population, a percentage much lower than official estimates[26].

It would appear that in absolute numbers there were more elderly persons residing in long-term care institutions at the turn of the century than there were at any other time over the next forty years despite the fact that the elderly population had trebled. As a proportion of the elderly population, institutional rates were half as great through the 1960s and early 1970s.

Although it is dangerous to speculate on the reasons for the higher rates at the turn of the century, it can be tentatively concluded or at least hypothesized, that families then were either less able or less willing to care for their elderly relations than presently. This is, of course, a simplistic conclusion drawn from a complex set of social factors. Relatively more institutional places were available then and it is possible that families today are neither more willing nor capable. Rather there are fewer places available. The data presented are demand statistics, effective demand, and are not to be confused with need. They only demonstrate what the long-term institutional population has been, is, and what it might be if present utilization rates continue. This point will be dealt with extensively in Chapters 5 and 6.

Community-based care

The preceding section has described trends in the utilization of services that can be characterized as a complete transfer of the caring function to the State, services that substitute for the family. This population, however, respresents only a fraction of the elderly. Ninety-seven per cent of the elderly are not institutionalized in long-term care facilities. The majority of the non-institutionalized elderly live with just their spouses (40 per cent), 26 per cent live alone, 19 per cent are living with their children and 15 per cent with others.

Since 1948 the State has developed a set of social policies that attempt to support the elderly in the community environment and either prevent or delay admission to long-term care settings. Two policy objectives are usually offered. The first argues that it is in the best interest of the elderly person and the family. The family is recognized as the primary support system, the social institution most suited to carry the major caring responsibility, the most natural social environment. The function of the social welfare system is seen as complementing the family through supportive social services. A second objective usually cited is that community care will prove less costly to the State in the long term.

The development of the community based social welfare services, such as the home help service, the provision of meals, the deployment of health visitors, home nurses, social workers, the provision of aids and adaptations, are all examples of the State attempting to support the elderly in the community. The underlying philosophy is that by partially substituting for the family through a transfer of various 'family functions', both the elderly person and the family will benefit.

While the home help service was greatly expanded following the Second World War, its beginnings go back seventy years. At the turn of the century a number of charitable organizations were providing help for mothers in the later stages of pregnancy, and childbirth. By 1931 41 of 131 local authorities in England and Wales had initiated a service. The major growth period followed the National Health Services Act of 1946 and the development of the Domestic Help Service under the administration of local health departments[27]. In 1968 the Government made the service compulsory.

The National Health Service Act also required local health authorities to provide for health visiting[28] and home nursing[29], and that these services be not limited to mothers and young children, but be made available to the family as a whole[30]. Finally, local authorities were given powers to make financial contributions to voluntary organizations for the provision of meals, chiropody, and laundry services[32].

Table 3.16 *Utilization trends — selected community services, rates per 1,000 elderly, 1958–73, England and Wales*

	Home helps		Health visiting		Home nursing		Meals on wheels
Year	Cases	w.t.e.	Cases	w.t.e.	Cases	w.t.e.	Weekly rates
1958	37.5	4.1	—	—	—	—	—
1959	39.9	4.3	—	—	—	—	—
1967	55.9	4.9	57.2	0.9	77.5	1.4	13.8
1968	57.6	4.9	58.3	0.9	81.9	1.4	15.6
1969	60.3	4.7	60.2	0.9	89.9	1.4	16.4
1970	62.3	4.7	63.0	0.9	90.2	1.4	17.7
1971	—	—	71.0	1.0	95.9	1.5	18.4
1972	67.1	5.3	—	(1.0)	—	1.5	20.5
1973	70.5	5.6	—	(1.0)	—	1.6	23.1

Notes: w.t.e. — whole-time equivalent.
Due to changes in definitions, figures for health visiting and home nursing (1972–73) are not comparable to earlier years and have not been included.

Sources: Annual Reports of the Ministry of Health, later the Department of Health and Social Security; and *Health and Personal Social Service Statistics for England.*

Home help service   Over a twenty-year period, 1953—73, the number of elderly receiving home help services grew from 115,000 to approximately 450,000, an increase of almost 300 per cent[33]. Since these figures are for 'cases', the actual number of elderly receiving the service is in fact much higher. However, the rate of increase has not been linear but has come in spurts. From 1953 to 1959, the average annual growth rate in home help cases was 12 per cent compared to 6 per cent for the years 1967 to 1973. From 1958 to 1973, the utilization rate grew from 37 per 1,000 elderly to 70 per 1,000.

This growth in commitment to domiciliary care has to be tempered somewhat because of the slower growth on the manpower side. The three-fold increase in cases (1953—73) has been accompanied by an increase of home helps (whole-time equivalents) of only 158 per cent. What becomes slightly disturbing is the fact that the highest period of growth in the home help services was the earlier period (1953—59) which showed an average annual increase of home help in the order of 8 per cent compared to 4 per cent from 1967 to 1973. In practice this has meant that each home help has had to provide services to significantly more cases than her counterpart in the preceding decade. In 1953, each home help on the average provided care to eight households. By 1973, twenty years later, the average caseload had grown to twelve. To put it another way, at the national level, each percentage increase in home help manpower was associated with an increase of almost two percentage points in users.

Health visiting   It is difficult to present trend data on the health visiting service. From 1951 to 1959 statistics reported on dealt with the number of visits. From 1965 to 1971 the reporting unit was changed to the number of cases or persons receiving the services. During the earlier period the volume of visits remained fairly constant, approximately 11 million each year. Over 87 per cent of all visits were made to mothers and children. In the later period, the number of active cases stabilized at 4.5 million annually. The major shift between the decades of the 1950s and 1960s was the growth in the number of elderly recipients. In 1965 these numbered 286,000; by 1971 the elderly using the health visiting services had increased to 454,000 (a growth of 60 per cent). As a percentage of the total user group, the elderly represent 10 per cent of the total, a slight increase over the decade. While the use rate by the elderly has increased each year since 1967, the manpower rate has remained constant.

Home nursing   From 1951 to 1959 the average annual caseload was approximately 1 million with a range of 1,177,000 in 1953 to 970,000 in 1959. By 1954 more than half of all visits were to elderly persons and since then each year has shown a gradual increase in this ratio. From 1967 to 1971 the number of all cases increased by 29 per cent, the number of elderly cases by 31 per cent and the number of full-time home nurses by

14 per cent. Over the last five years reported (1967–71) for each unit increase in manpower, there was a 2 per cent increase in the number of cases, a pattern similar to developments in the home help services.

Meals service   Over a seven-year period (1967–73) the total volume of meals provided to the elderly increased by 84 per cent, from 15 to 28 million meals. Two of every three of these meals were delivered to the homes of the elderly, the remainder provided in lunch clubs and day centres. The Department of Health and Social Security recommended in 1970 that the elderly be encouraged to take their meals at clubs and centres rather than in their homes, and since then there has been a shift in this direction[34]. While the increase in the number of home meals was approximately 68 per cent since 1967, the number of recipients increased by 87 per cent. In spite of volume increase, utilization outstripped supply and well over half of all recipients received two or fewer meals per week.

Sheltered housing   The concept of grouped sheltered housing for the elderly has only surfaced in the United Kingdom over the past thirty years. These schemes, incorporating a warden and communication system as well as special design features, have been proposed as a viable alternative for many of the elderly who are disabled or infirm. The rationale behind such a social service is that the sheltered housing offers a more normal social environment than the usual residential care facilities and has a therapeutic benefit in that the elderly are encouraged to do as much as they can for themselves. The setting is not fully institutional, yet the necessary support services are provided, including probably the most critical of all – the presence and interest of a caring person. Townsend reported that in 1958, 4,300 such units had been built giving a rate of 9 per 100,000 elderly. He further suggested a target of 5,000 per 100,000 elderly[35]. Currently there are approximately 50,000 such units in existence or 100 per 100,000 elderly, a considerable improvement but far short of the projected 350,000 that are necessary[36].

Implications   There is no question as to the considerable increases in the community based services. The growth in volume has exceeded the increases in the elderly population. However, the fact is that increases in manpower have been considerably lower than increases in the number of recipients. What are the implications of these trends? Has broader coverage been achieved through greater productivity on the part of the home helps and in general a more effective organization, or has it been possible only by providing less service to more people?

Harris in her study on the needs of the elderly reports evidence to support the latter. Home help organizers were asked what policy they would follow if demand increased. In one local authority they responded

Table 3.17 *Per cent increase in utilization of selected community services and whole-time equivalent manpower, 1967–71, England and Wales*

Service	Utilization	w.t.e. manpower
Home helps	19	10
Health visiting	37	18
Home nursing	31	14
Chiropody	22	39

Source: DHSS, *Health and Personal Social Service Statistics for England*, HMSO, 1974, pp. 107, 108, 110, 115.

that they 'might have to cut the number of hours but would not withdraw the home help completely'[37]. 'In one area the policy is to give the least possible amount of help for the shortest time, while in another, the policy is to give as much help as is necessary to keep the home the way the old person would keep it if she were able to do her own housekeeping'[38]. Harris reached the conclusion that the amount of time given by the home help did not depend on the needs of the elderly requiring the service. On the average recipients received three to four hours per week, with a range of one to ten hours. These findings are corroborated by a later survey of the home help service carried out by Hunt[39].

Pasker and Ashley in their study of the frail elderly found that 64 per cent were receiving home help services, averaging four hours per week, but that receipt of the service was inversely related to need[40]. In relative terms, those with the greatest need received the least amount of service. Finally Townsend and Wedderburn in their national survey found that of the small number of elderly receiving home help support, 71 per cent received two or less visits per week. Interestingly, this survey was carried out in 1963 when the ratio of home help to cases was significantly higher than current ratios[41].

Similar patterns are found in the other domiciliary services. Sumner and Smith concluded that 'over 45 per cent of the patients were not receiving the nursing then needed'[42]. Harris in her interviews with general practitioners found them dissatisfied with the amount of home nursing provided in eleven of the twelve areas studied[43].

In spite of the fact that utilization has increased, rates among the handicapped elderly are disturbing: 37 per cent of the very severely handicapped, 56 per cent of the severely handicapped, and 70 per cent of the impaired were not receiving any of the basic community social welfare services. The fact that the very severely handicapped received fewer home help and meals services than the severely handicapped can be partially explained by the fact that they were more likely to be living with their children, a criterion that appears to affect utilization.

Table 3.18   *Utilization of community services by the handicapped elderly, 1968, Great Britain (percentages)*

	Very severe	Severe	Appreci- able	Im- paired	All elderly 1968
Health visitors	12.1	7.0	4.0	4.0	5.8
Home nurses	40.0	13.0	8.0	7.0	7.7
Home helps	13.6	17.0	11.0	7.0	5.8
Meals on wheels	3.6	5.0	3.0	2.0	1.6
Social workers	10.6	7.0	4.0	4.0	–
Chiropodists	17.0	17.0	12.0	11.0	13.0
None	37.0	56.0	68.0	72.0	–

Source: Harris, *Handicapped and Impaired in Great Britain*, OPCS, Social Survey Division, HMSO, 1971, p. 50.

Hunt found that 71 per cent of recipients of the home help service were living alone and only 2.2 per cent of recipients were living with their children[44]. Wager found that 72 per cent of home help recipients lived alone and of those elderly who lived with children, none received home help or meals and only 4 per cent were receiving home nursing services[45]. There is a recurring theme throughout studies on utilization of community services: elderly people living alone or with their spouses are much more likely to be provided with help. If the elderly person is living with relatives, especially children, the service is withheld on the assumption that the family will provide needed care. In other situations, it would appear that even when family members cannot or will not provide care, the service is refused on the basis that they should do so. In practice, then, some local authorities are still guided by the principle of family responsibility as enunciated in 43rd Eliz.

Discussion

Based on this analysis of utilization data, it can be concluded that there is no clear evidence that the State is assuming the primary responsibility for the care of the elderly. If the analysis were restricted to patterns of institutionalization the opposite would seem to emerge. Earlier it was proposed that long-term institutional care — the transfer of complete responsibility — might be used as a viable surrogate indicator of a broader trend. Yet current rates of institutionalization are significantly lower than those of the first three decades of this century.

Since 1951 the number and percentage of elderly living in long-term care institutions has increased considerably, but even in this case, the increase is directly related to the changing age structure of the elderly population. More elderly are over eighty-four years of age, and it is this group that has the highest rates of institutionalization. In spite of the higher institutional rates among this age group 91 per cent of males and 88 per cent of females are living in non-institutional settings.

It must be emphasized, however, that institutional rates are a function of a number of complex factors. The data presented represent effective demand and cannot under any stretch of the imagination be viewed as a sensitive indicator of need. Each year, as additional places have been made available, the numbers have increased. If more residential care facilities were to be built, the utilization rates would inevitably rise, partially because of unmet need, partially for financial reasons, since empty beds often mean economic loss, and possibly because increase in the supply of places will stimulate new demand.

The data on the domiciliary services is less conclusive. These services, in which there is a partial transfer of the caring function to the social welfare system and in which some 'family functions' are taken over, are being used at much higher rates. Each year since 1953 has shown a greater percentage of elderly using these services. However, the allocation of resources to the community services has lagged considerably. While the domiciliary services have been proposed as a meaningful alternative to institutional care, a

Table 3.19   *Trends in social welfare expenditure for selected services — percentages by service, 1958—71, England and Wales*

	Residen- tial care	Home helps	Health visiting	Home nursing	Total (£ '000s)
1958–59	41	26	12	21	36.5
1964–65	47	23	11	18	60.9
1965–66	46	24	11	19	67.6
1966–67	54	16	11	19	75.8
1967–68	52	19	11	18	88.2
1968–69	51	20	11	18	93.9
1969–70	50	22	11	17	101.2
1970–71	49	23	11	17	121.0
Average 1964–65/ 1970–71	50	21	11	18	

Notes: Figures are for net expenditure at current prices on all population groups (excluding residential care where calculations were only for elderly). Therefore these are overestimates on expenditures for the aged. The elderly have made up between 75 and 85 per cent of all home help cases; 50 to 56 per cent of the home nursing cases; and 8 to 10 per cent of the health visiting cases. It is impossible to estimate their share of the expenditures however, since this would involve a breakdown by time given to each user group.

Sources: Annual Reports of the Ministry of Health, later the Department of Health and Social Security; and *Health and Personal Social Service Statistics for England.*

review of expenditure patterns would suggest they have been assigned unequal status.

In 1958–59, expenditures on residential care represented 41 per cent of all expenditures on these core services; the home help service represented 26 per cent. It should be remembered that it was at this time that the concept of community care had just begun to emerge as a policy priority. Since then the share of the budget given to residential care has increased and quite possibly at the expense of the other services. Between 1964 and 1971, for every pound spent on residential care for the elderly, 42 pence was expended on the home help service; 22 pence on health visiting; and 36 pence on home nursing. This analysis is not designed to suggest that there is a fixed amount of resources to be divided among these service components and that an increase in one will automatically result in a decrease in another; rather, the argument is that patterns of expenditure can be analysed to determine implicit priorities in policies. While the explicit policy since 1959 may have emphasized community services, experience since then suggests that the policy is less than meaningful. As recently as 1972–73, 60 per cent of all local authority personal social service expenditure in England went to residential care (£107 million) compared to 23 per cent for the home help service (£40 million)[46].

Institutional care usually represents the complete transfer of the caring function to the State and is fundamentally a residual approach to social welfare. In a small percentage of cases the institution is used on a short-term basis to provide relief to the family. The norm is, however, long-term care. The State intervenes when the elderly person can no longer function, has no family, or whose family is either unable or unwilling to provide the necessary support. This group has and will continue to receive the highest priority among the elderly even though they represent less than 3 per cent of the elderly population. Furthermore, this will continue to be made possible at the expense of the non-institutionalized elderly since it will probably result in less growth in the community services.

This imbalance has created a number of problems. Demand for the domiciliary services has increased faster than resources and recipients are being provided less services than in the past, whether this is the number of hours per week of home help and home nursing or the number of meals per week. Accompanying this is a trend among providers of service to establish priorities among potential users. Elderly who live alone or just with their spouses are more likely to receive services while those who live with their children or within an extended kin network are more likely to be denied help.

This practice has been defended on grounds of economic efficiency. Scarce resources are channelled to those with the greatest need. In doing so, however, the State is operating on the principle of intervention only when the family cannot or will not provide care. The State still becomes the substitute family in the same way it does when an elderly person enters an institution. The major difference is that the transfer is not complete.

These policies implicitly recognize the existence of both the nuclear and extended family unit. To some degree the State becomes the extended family network for the elderly nuclear family by providing certain help. It also withholds services when a network is believed to exist. It is possible that in making this policy distinction, the State is actually penalizing those families who are willing to retain the primary caring function. By not offering support, existing social policy might actually force many families to give up this function prematurely, given the evidence of the severe strain many families are experiencing. If this were to happen, the family and the State would not be sharing the responsibility through an inter-dependent relationship and it is conceivable that eventually, the social welfare system would be pressured with demands to provide even greater amounts of care, to become the family for more and more elderly persons.

These issues will be discussed at greater length in Chapters 5 and 6. What is clear is that the majority of the elderly do have a family network offering support. Most of these families are willing to provide care in spite of the fact that operating social policies appear to neglect their effort. Over the next twenty to thirty years families, under present policy, will be required to do even more, given the projected increases in the number and age structure of this 'at risk' population.

Townsend concluded over ten years ago:

There is little evidence of health and welfare services being 'misused' or 'undermining' family responsibilities. Those who benefit from the services are mainly infirm or incapacitated persons who lack a family or have none within reach. This suggests that the family does in fact play a positive role for many old people, and a considerable body of data support this suggestion[47].

While this appears to be the case still, it is only one aspect of the policy issue. The State may not have taken responsibility from the family but has it consciously taken steps to strengthen the family? Does it encourage the family to continue to function as the primary social service?

References

1. Throughout this report the term 'elderly' usually refers to the popula-tion (male and female) over sixty-four years of age. The data in Table 3.2 is one of the few exceptions. Here the elderly are males sixty-five years and over and females sixty years and over.

2. A. Harris, (*a*) *Social Welfare for the Elderly*, GSS, HMSO, 1968, and (*b*) *Handicapped and Impaired in Great Britain*, OPCS, Social Survey Division, HMSO, 1971; A. Hunt, *The Home Help Service in England*

and Wales, GSS, HMSO, 1970. For a comprehensive discussion of the shortfalls in services for the elderly see DHSS Circular 35/72.

3. For example, see: M. Meacher 'The old: the future of community care', and J. Agate, 'The old: hospital and community care', in *The Fifth Social Service: A Critical Analysis of the Seebohm proposals*, Civic Press Limited, Fabian Society, 1970; N. Bosanquet, *New deal for the elderly*, Fabian Tract 435, The Fabian Society, 1975.

4. The actual expenditures are much higher but impossible to delineate; e.g. housing expenditures on this group.

5. For a listing of surveys on the aged carried out between 1945 and 1963 see: P. Townsend and D. Wedderburn, *The Aged in the Welfare State*, Bell, 1965, Appendix 1, pp. 140–3.

6. E. Shanas *et al. Old People in Three Industrial Societies*, Routledge and Kegan Paul, 1968 (the results of this survey were also reported in P. Townsend and D. Wedderburn, op. cit. (ref. 5); A. Harris, op. cit. (ref. 2); OPCS, Social Survey Division, *The General Household Survey*, HMSO, 1973.

7. See: E. Shanas *et al.* op. cit., pp. 26–30 for a discussion of the Index of Incapacity.

8. A. Harris, op. cit. (ref. 2b), p. 2.

9. OPCS, *The General Household Survey*, p. 264.

10. A. Harris, op. cit. (ref. 2b), pp. 4–5.

11. Ibid., pp. 26–7.

12. E. Shanas *et al.*, op. cit. (ref. 6), p. 21.

13. GSS, CSO, *Social Trends, 1974*, HMSO, 1974, p. 91. The elderly include men sixty-five years of age and over and women sixty years of age and over. Unfortunately it is not possible to include only the over sixty-four group.

14. General Register Office, *Sample Census*, HMSO, 1966.

15. E. Shanas *et al.*, op. cit. (ref. 6), pp. 196, 205.

16. While there are no similar national surveys there are a number of smaller studies that document the extent of care provided by families. See for example: D. Kettle and L. Hart, *Health of the Elderly Project*, London, King Edward Hospital Fund, 1974; Coventry Social Services, *Looking for Trouble*, 1973.

17. A. Harris, op. cit. (ref. 2b), p. 69.

18. Ibid., pp. 13–16.

19. P. Sainsbury and J. Grad de Alarcon, 'The psychiatrist and the geriatric patient: the effects of community care on the family of the geriatric patient', *Journal of Geriatric Psychiatry*, 4, no. 1, 1971, 23–41.

20. C. Lowther and J. Williamson, 'Old people and their relatives'. *The Lancet*, 31 December 1966.

21. J. Cresswell and P. Pasker, 'The frail who lead the frail', *New Society*, 25 May 1972, pp. 407–10.

22. M. Anderson, *Family Structure in Nineteenth Century Lancashire*, Cambridge University Press, 1971, p. 178.

23. M. Rosenheim, 'Social welfare and its implications for family living', in *Social Structure and the Family: Generational Relations*, eds, E. Shanas and G. Streib, Prentice-Hall, 1965, p. 213.

24. P. Townsend and D. Wedderburn, op. cit. (ref. 5), p. 171; R. Wager, *Care of the Elderly*, London, Institute of Municipal Treasurers and Accountants, 1972, p. 16; E. Goldberg, *Helping the Aged*, Allen and Unwin, 1970.

25. P. Townsend and D. Wedderburn, op. cit. (ref. 5); H. Wager, op. cit. (ref. 24); E. Goldberg, op. cit. (ref. 24); A. Harris, op. cit. (ref. 2a).

26. For example, the DHSS estimates that local authorities should plan 25 places per 1,000 elderly population in residential care accommodations. These estimates are based on 1971 utilization (21 per 1,000, which includes private residential places).

27. National Health Service Act, 1946, Part III, s. 29.

28. National Health Service Act, 1946, Part III, s. 24.

29. National Health Service Act, 1946, Part III, s. 25.

30. Ministry of Health, Circular 118/47.

31. National Assistance Act, 1948, Part III, s. 31.

32. For example: National Assistance Act, 1948; the Mental Health Act, 1959; National Assistance Act, 1962; Health Visitors and Social Work Training Act, 1962; Health Services and Public Health Act, 1968; Chronically Sick and Disabled Persons Act, 1970; Local Authority Personal Social Services Act, 1970.

33. These numbers cover only England since data for England and Wales is not available for 1972–73.

34. DHSS Circular 5/70.

35. P. Townsend, *The Last Refuge*, Routledge and Kegan Paul, 1962.

36. N. Bosanquet, op. cit. (ref. 3), p. 11.

37. A. Harris, op. cit. (ref. 2a), p. 13.

38. Ibid., p. 66.

39. A. Hunt, op. cit. (ref. 2).

40. P. Pasker and J. Ashley, 'Interrelationship of different sectors of the total health and social services system', *Community Medicine*, **126**, no. 20, 1971, 272–6.

41. P. Townsend and D. Wedderburn, op. cit. (ref. 5).

42. G. Sumner and R. Smith, *Planning Local Authority Services for the Elderly*, Allen and Unwin, 1969.

43. A. Harris, op. cit. (ref. 2a).

44. A. Hunt, op. cit. (ref. 2), pp. 238—41.

45. R. Wager, op. cit. (ref. 24), pp. 30—2.

46. DHSS statistics reported by N. Bosanquet, op. cit. (ref. 3), p. 8.

47. P. Townsend and D. Wedderburn, op. cit. (ref. 5), p. 135.

4 The family and the mentally handicapped child

The severely mentally handicapped are another 'high risk' dependent group who have made and will continue to make heavy demands on both the family and the social welfare system. In the previous chapter it was pointed out that the ageing process is irreversible. Similarly, severe mental handicap can be viewed as a non-curable condition. This statement, however, requires both clarification and qualification. Mental handicap as such is a functional designation, that applies at the time at which an assessment is made. There is ample evidence that with appropriate and adequate intervention the degree of handicap can be altered, and physical, social, and intellectual functioning can be improved. Still, it is unlikely that a severely mentally handicapped person will improve to the point that he would no longer be designated as mentally handicapped.

While there are similarities between these two groups, the aged and the mentally handicapped, there are a number of significant differences that justify a separate analysis. The issue of family care and family responsibility is fundamental to both, but the dimensions of the caring function are not the same. Most people lead normal lives (in the sense of physical, emotional and social wellbeing) before they become elderly, and old age is considered to be a natural stage in the life cycle. Technological advances, in the broad sense, have produced an environment in which the great majority of the population will live beyond the age of sixty-five, the artificial but historical point between middle age and old age. Currently, survival into old age is viewed both individually and societally as one criterion of modern success. For some, old age will mean physical limitation, social isolation, and economic hardship but these are a minority of the elderly, albeit a large minority. Unfortunately, many studies emphasize the associated problems and needs — unfortunate in the sense that they distort the status of most old people. Many elderly are handicapped, disadvantaged, and in critical need of support. However, if these figures are turned around, the fact is that 75 per cent of all elderly are not living alone, 95 per cent are not socially isolated, 75 per cent are not impaired and 90 per cent are not handicapped[1]. The recently published survey on the attitudes of the elderly undertaken by Age Concern provides strong evidence that for most people, old age is a positive experience[2]. The care of an elderly parent, especially the frail elderly, can bring about heavy strains, but compared to other groups of socially dependent requiring care, the time involved is relatively short and family members know that eventually, a matter of years at most, the elderly member will die. Another difference should also be noted. As pointed out in Chapter 2, the primary care provider — the daughter of the elderly parent — usually assumes this role after she has raised her family and has been free to work. In most cases, the family has led a 'normal life' before these new demands are made.

The situation is quite different for families who have a severely mentally handicapped child. Like the elderly, the increase in numbers is the result of technological advances and improved standards of living. Previously many of the severely handicapped would not have survived. Now the severely handicapped child can be expected not only to survive childhood, but the majority will live an adult life. Whereas increased longevity for the aged is a successful outcome, for the mentally handicapped and their families, the success is only partial. Families, especially parents, are not faced with the prospect of providing care for a matter of years after a 'normal life', but for decades. For these families the idea of a normal life has to be redefined. While those family members caring for an elderly relative can anticipate picking up their life after the relative dies, parents with mentally handicapped children know well that probably they will be survived by them. Finally, ageing is perceived as natural while a mental handicap is not.

This chapter discusses briefly what mental retardation is, the size of the affected population, and the characteristics of the mentally handicapped. Their needs and the needs of their families are then explored in some detail. Finally, patterns of social care and trends in the provision of social welfare services are identified.

Historical background and definitional problems

One of the major problems facing the analyst concerned with the mentally handicapped is that an historical data base does not exist. In the previous chapter it was possible to identify the number of people defined as elderly at various points over the past 175 years. Within normal sampling and reporting errors found in the ongoing decennial census various rates could be generated and reasonably strong inferences could be extrapolated dealing with trends in patterns of social care provision.

The situation is not the same with the mentally handicapped. Over the past 150 years there has not been an ongoing census of handicapped and the condition itself has gone through a series of definitional changes making comparisons extremely difficult. Despite this problem it is still useful to trace historical developments in so far as they provide some idea of how society has viewed the mentally handicapped and the patterns of care that have evolved.

Very little systematic information on the mentally handicapped had been collected during the first half of the nineteenth century. In fact there was scarcely any mention of this group in the Poor Law Report of 1832. In 1881, a survey of 'idiots', a group that included mental defectives of any grade, found slightly under 30,000 individuals currently in public institutions; less than 1,000 of these were residents of mental deficiency institutions: the rest were located in various work houses, lunatic asylums and prisons[3]. While the total number of mental defectives was unknown, the institutional rate was estimated to be 1.13 per 1,000 population.

In the latter half of the nineteenth century, a consensus emerged that segregation of the mentally handicapped was the most desirable policy. The Idiots Act, 1886, permitted local authorities to build special institutions for this group[4], and in a relatively short period of time this permissive legislation became the usual practice. Sandlebridge Colony was established in 1898 on the principle that 'the children to be cared for are to be detained for the whole of their lives ... only permanent care could be really efficacious in stemming the great evil of feeblemindedness in our country'[5]. At the turn of the century, the members of the Poor Law Commission, alarmed by 'an army [of mental defectives] approaching 200,000 in number, more than one-sixth of the entire pauper host' re-affirmed that: 'In England and Wales it is, speaking generally, the County or County Borough Council acting through its Asylums Committee, which is the Local Lunacy Committee, *charged by statutes* [emphasis added], to make the necessary institutional provision for persons certified to be of unsound mind'[6].

The Eugenics movement, led by Sir Francis Galton and eventually supported by the National Association for the Care of the Feeble-Minded (NACF), took the position that the condition was inherited and nothing could be done effectively to treat the mentally handicapped. Lifelong segregation and a public policy of sterilization of the 'unfit' was seen as the only practical solution. It was in the interest of both the defective person and society.

By 1910 the NACF estimated that there were 270,000 mentally defective people in England and Wales, giving a rate of 7.5 per 1,000 population; 45 per cent, or 121,000 had been 'certified' while 149,000 were not. In 1920 the Board of Control estimated there were 135,000 mentally defective persons in England and Wales or 3.5 per 1,000 population, of whom slightly over 10,000 had been 'ascertained'. The Report of the Wood Committee, 1929, in many respects one of the most valuable of these earlier reports, added to the confusion by estimating that there were 33,000 mentally defective children between the ages of seven and sixteen or 6 per 1,000 in this population. Two members of the Committee disagreed and suggested the rates were closer to 8 per 1,000 population. Further they estimated the number of adult mentally defective to be 175,000 giving a number of 225,000 excluding children under the age of seven, or 6 per 1,000[7].

Over a thirty-year period, then, from 1900–30, the estimated rates of mental deficiency ranged from 3.5 per 1,000 to almost 8 per 1,000 population. Part of this problem was due to the fact that definitions were vague or had changed, and to the absence of measurable criteria. In 1890, under the Lunacy Act, a mental defective was either an idiot or a person of unsound mind. In practice, the labelling of an individual as defective was the subjective judgment of the examiner. By 1903 many local authorities decided whether an individual was mentally deficient on the basis of a literacy test, despite the fact that compulsory education was fairly new. Galton, a few years later, defined a mentally defective person as 'mad, idiotic, or feeble-minded'[8]. The rates quoted above, estimating between 100,000 and 300,000 mentally handicapped are quite suspect. A large number of these in all probability would be diagnosed as mentally ill today. Also, no distinction was made as to the severity of the mental handicap. A significant number classified as defective were likely to be minimally handicapped, a category that shifts over time.

The Mental Deficiency Act of 1913 attempted to resolve the problem and proposed four categories of mental deficiency: idiots, imbeciles, feeble-minded and moral defectives[9]. Only one, feeble-mindedness, was based on an educational criterion (and even here only in the case of children) while the others were primarily based on an assessment as to whether the individual was a threat to himself or to others. While the Act did attempt to clarify what mental deficiency actually covered, few criteria were operational and the line between mental illness, mental deficiency, and normality remained blurred.

The next thirty years saw a continuous debate over two key issues: the criteria to be used in diagnosing mental deficiency and the methods for the care of those so identified. The Wood Committee (1929) recommended that criteria should be based more on social functioning than on educational skills and intelligence testing. While most agreed that mental deficiency should not be based solely on intelligence tests, little agreement could be found as to what constituted social functioning, let alone how it should be measured. Even after the passage of the Mental Health Act of 1959, in which subnormality of intelligence was included in a broader definition of mental subnormality, the issue was still unresolved[10]. In practice, intelligence (as measured by tests) is still the dominant criterion. The Wood Committee further recommended that greater emphasis should be placed on community care and yet, in 1946, the government was strongly advised to double the existing number of institutional places from 46,000 to 92,000[11].

This brief analysis has highlighted the confusion surrounding the issue of mental handicap in the latter half of the nineteenth century and the first half of the present century. Mental deficiency itself was not understood, and definitions changed time and time again producing great fluctuations in prevalence estimates. Despite the implicit suggestions of the Elementary Education Act of 1899 and the explicit recommendations of the Wood Committee thirty years later to provide services in the community, usual practice continued to be the segregation of the mentally handicapped in state institutions.

Of equal importance was the general reaction of society to the families of the mentally handicapped. Since mental deficiency was believed to be inherited, the prevailing view was that parents and siblings were likely to be mentally defective themselves. The prevailing sentiment encouraged segregation and sterilization for the protection of society, and there appears to have been little discussion of providing support to families who might wish to provide care for the mentally handicapped in the home. There was little discussion of shared responsibility since the families themselves were viewed as incapable. Extreme as this sounds, it was a logical conclusion evolving from the official position of the Eugenics' Society and the NACF. Even after the influence of these organizations lessened, segregation remained the dominant pattern of care and it was only in the 1950s that attention began to shift to the needs of the families of mentally handicapped and the desirability of community care.

The prevalence of mental handicap

The 1960s brought some degree of order to this definitional chaos. Earlier classification systems using such terminology as idiot, imbecile, feeble-mindedness and mental deficiency were discarded. In the United States the American Association on Mental Deficiency (AAMD) developed a classification in 1959 and revised it in 1961. The President's Panel on Mental Retardation adopted this nomenclature in 1962. The World Health Organization (WHO) in 1968 proposed four categories to be used in classifying the degree of mental handicap: profound (IQ less than 20); severe (IQ 20–35); moderate (IQ 35–50); and mild (IQ 50–70). The major difference between this classification system and that developed by the AAMD was the exclusion of a fifth category — borderline mental retardation, a category that contained a larger number of handicapped than the other four categories combined. The AAMD accepted the rationale offered by WHO and eliminated the borderline group in 1973. In England the preferred term for mental deficiency became mental handicap, and two categories were developed: severe subnormality (IQ less than 50) and subnormality (IQ 50–70).

While the same criticisms could be made of this classification system based on intelligence testing that were made earlier, Tizard has argued that:

For epidemiological purposes the value of assessing grade or severity of mental handicap in terms of IQ is very great. . . . Moreover, well established epidemiological findings indicate that the traditional distinction between idiots and imbeciles or severely retarded persons on the one hand, and morons, feeble-minded or mildly retarded persons on the other, is a meaningful one biologically and socially[12].

This study is primarily concerned with the severely handicapped and fortunately there seems to be reasonable agreement here among epidemiologists on the issue of prevalence rates.

Based on these studies, the Department of Health and Social Security has assumed a prevalence rate of between 2 and 3 per 1,000 population, or an estimated 120,000 people with severe mental handicap in 1971[13].

The peak prevalence rate is estimated at 3.6 per 1,000 persons aged fifteen to nineteen. Tizard has suggested that this prevalence rate is probably close to the true prevalence rates for all age groups up to fifteen in so far as severe mental handicap is almost always present from birth or early infancy[14]. If this rate were applied to the total population under fifteen years of age, there would have been slightly over 42,000 severely handicapped children in England and Wales in 1971.

Table 4.1   *Estimated prevalence of severe mental handicap, 1951—2001, England and Wales ('000s)*

Year	Under 15	15 and over	Total
1951	35	74	109
1961	38	77	115
1971	42	80	122
1981	42	85	127
1991	44	88	132
2001	46	92	138

Note: The rates used were: for the population under fifteen years of age, 3.6 per 1,000; for the population over fourteen, 2.2 per 1,000, giving a total prevalence rate of 2.5 per 1,000.

Sources: Population figures for 1951—71 were derived from appropriate OPCS, *Census Reports*, General Register Office. Projected population figures for 1981—2001 were derived from the CSU, *Annual Abstract of Statistics, 1972, No. 109*, HMSO, Table 15, p. 16.

The data covering 1951—71 are derived from the survey results cited above and projections for the next thirty years assume that the rates will remain constant. One of every three severely subnormal were estimated to be children. The projections for the next thirty years are based on extremely conservative assumptions. They begin with Tizard's position that prevalence among children is not increasing substantially[15] and with the Department of Health and Social Security's current view that the possibilities of preventing severe mental subnormality are limited at present[16], although others are more optimistic, especially in terms of spina bifida, Down's Syndrome and birth traumas. The projections further assume that the ratio of children to adults will remain constant at 1:2, but this is highly suspect. Tizard suggests that 'since many more severely handicapped children survive to adult life, the *number* of adult retardates *are* increasing'[17]. Therefore the rate of 2.2 per 1,000 for the population over fourteen years of age will possibly be higher. Despite these caveats, the figures are useful, especially those for the population under fifteen years of age. They offer reasonable estimates and can be used in analysing trends for services and patterns of care.

Characteristics of the severely mentally handicapped

As a condition severe mental handicap is usually associated with gross structural damage to the brain and neurological abnormalities. It is not found disproportionately in one social class over another and while parents are rarely 'defective', siblings occasionally are. Prognosis includes a reduced expectation of life and lifelong dependency[18].

A number of studies have shown that the condition is strongly correlated with a broad range of physical disorders, such as epilepsy, visual, hearing and speech defects[19]. Table 4.2 gives estimates of type and degree of physical and behaviour difficulties associated with severe mental subnormality. Though drawn from careful surveys in Wessex, Newcastle and Camberwell, the Department of Health and Social Security cautions that the data should be 'interpreted as broad indications rather than precise findings'[20].

Table 4.2 *Incapacity associated with severe mental handicap*

Incapacity	Under 15	15 and over	Total
Non-ambulant	24.06	6.23	11.45
Behaviour difficulties requiring constant supervision	14.06	11.23	12.06
Severely incontinent	12.55	5.20	7.34
Needing assistance to feed, wash, and dress	28.33	15.49	19.25
No physical handicap or severe behaviour difficulties	21.00	61.85	49.90
	(100.00)	(100.00)	(100.00)

Sources: Adapted from DHSS, *Better Services for the Mentally Handicapped*, Cmnd 4683, HMSO, 1971, Table I, p. 6.

One of every two severely mentally handicapped persons (both children and adults) were found to have neither a physical handicap nor a severe behaviour problem. One of every five needed assistance in personal care functions; one in eight had severe behavioural problems; one in nine was non-ambulant; and one in fourteen was severely incontinent. However, incapacity is clearly associated with age. With the exception of behaviour difficulties the handicapped under the age of fifteen were more likely to be disabled. Children were twice as likely to be incontinent and to need assistance with personal care functions, and four times more likely to be non-ambulant. Four of every five mentally handicapped children were likely to have a physical handicap or severe behaviour problem compared to two of every five adults. A number of factors can be identified to explain at least a part of this difference. First is the fact that many of the very severely handicapped did not survive childhood. However, as cited above, the number surviving has increased and in time this will probably result in higher rates of incapacity among the older group. Second, many severely mentally handicapped children can be expected to acquire some personal care skills, including ambulation and bowel and bladder control.

Nevertheless the differences are significant. Based on a prevalence rate of 3.6 per 1,000 for this age group, 10,000 severely mentally handicapped children were estimated to be non-ambulant, 6,000 children to have severe behavioural problems, 5,000 incontinent and 12,000 needing assistance in personal care. Assuming that the distribution of severe mental handicap is similar to the age distribution in the general population, it can be estimated that roughly one-third will be under five years of age, one-third will be five to nine, and the rest ten to fourteen. All parents of children, handicapped or normal, accept the reality that they will be required to provide basic care in infancy. Problems of incontinence, personal care, and ambulation increase as the child grows and it is another matter to maintain care when the child is no longer an infant. The physical and emotional demands can be severe.

Effects of mental handicap on the family

The last section described the incapacities and disabilities associated with mental handicap. The presence of a mentally handicapped child is likely also to have a significant impact on other members of the family and on the family as a social unit. Some researchers have argued that parents of a handicapped child will experience severe strains often resulting in marital breakdown[21]. Parents have been described as both angry and guilt-ridden, angry that it happened to them and guilty in the sense that they are somehow responsible[22]. Finally, it has been suggested that many parents, unable to cope with these feelings, tend to blame their spouses[23]. The trauma that brings on bitterness, guilt and shame in turn contributes to serious emotional problems, quarrelling and, in a substantial number of cases, marital disintegration[24]. These findings, however, are partially contradicted by other researchers. Fowle in her study of families with severely handicapped children concluded that 'marital integration was not adversely affected'[25]. While it was indisputable that there were severe strains on the family, the majority developed a number of coping mechanisms[26]. If the studies are examined closely, part of these differences might be explained on the basis of the samples. The former, associated with a high prevalence of marital discord, were families who had come to agencies because they were experiencing problems in adjustment. The latter, on the other hand, were drawn from community surveys of families with handicapped members[27].

In spite of these differences there is general agreement among researchers that the presence of a severely mentally handicapped child is likely to seriously affect family life. One of the more critical effects is the high degree of social isolation. Holt in a study of 200 families reported that two of every three were 'noticeably isolated'; 74 per cent of the mothers felt that their neighbours objected to the handicapped child associating with their children[28]. Tizard and Grad found less than normal social contacts in 50 per cent of the 250 families in their survey and 15 per cent were 'severely limited' in their social contacts[29]. These findings are supported by a large number of other studies[30]. The parents felt stigmatized. Whether they were actually rejected by the community or in fact were choosing isolation is not clear.

Social isolation or diminished social interaction is only one dimension ‣of the stresses experienced by families. Family life was disrupted in almost every area. In some situations fathers found it necessary to modify their careers in the interest of the handicapped child; many families had less opportunity for holidays and recreational activities and found it necessary to adjust their plans considerably to suit the needs of the child[31]. Other families preferred to stay in cottages, caravans or with relatives rather than face the embarrassment of interacting with strangers[32]. Families also experienced serious housing and financial problems directly related to the presence of a mentally handicapped child[33].

Serious as these disruptions are, they represent only the tip of the iceberg. For most families it is the day-to-day strain and demand that concerns them most[34]. Many activities most people take for granted can become crises. Severely handicapped children often cannot be left alone for any length of time, yet to take a handicapped child shopping creates serious problems. Travelling on buses or trains can be extremely difficult, especially if the child becomes restless or has a behavioural problem. Handicapped children create extra work, especially in respect to feeding, dressing and bathing.

Child-rearing and associated daily demands can tax ordinary life but these families are not faced with time limited crises. The problems are complex and their impact cumulative. Often the mother's health is affected. Hewitt found that 14 per cent of the mothers in her study felt they were in poor health, 12 per cent 'run down', and 27 per cent in moderate health. Less than one-half stated they were in good health. Six out of every ten mothers said they suffered from feelings of depression[35]. Tizard and Grad reported on the unsatisfactory mental health of many parents in their survey[36]. A number of families felt that their normal children were experiencing problems, including role tension[37]. Holt found that some siblings resented the fact that the parents paid too much attention to the handicapped child and they were often embarrassed when interacting with their peers[38].

It is a gross understatement to say that these families are 'at risk'. The problems and demands they are experiencing are staggering. If there are transfers of the caring function from families to the State, it is likely to be found in these families. Throughout this century, especially the first sixty years, official policy has supported institutionalization, and families in all probability were encouraged by professionals to take this course. Families who did seek institutionalization were not stigmatized. In fact, the evidence seems to suggest the opposite. Families who decided to care for the mentally handicapped child felt isolated from the rest of the community. What has the pattern been?

Institutional trends

One major difficulty in attempting to document trends in institutional rates is the periodic shifts in the definition of what constitutes an institution for the mentally handicapped and what constitutes a mentally handicapped patient. From 1949 to 1960 the Ministry of Health published annual reports showing the number of residents in hospitals vested in the Ministry of Health, institutions legally designated to receive the 'mentally deficient'. Following the 1959 Mental Health Act, the Ministry altered the criteria to include all patients with a diagnosis of mental subnormality who were in National Health Service beds and under the care of a psychiatrist[39]. Rather than reporting just those numbers officially classified as institutionalized patients, the data for the earlier period includes those

Table 4.3   *Mentally handicapped patients in hospital care, 1952–71, England and Wales*

Year	Total patients	Rates per 1,000 pop.	Waiting list	Ratio of patients to those on waiting list
1952	58,289	1.32	—	—
1954	60,027	1.35	7,033	8:1
1955	60,634	1.36	6,909	9:1
1957	60,019	1.33	5,763	10:1
1959	60,469	1.32	5,918	10:1
1962	61,471	1.32	5,512	11:1
1963	64,622	1.38	5,300	12:1
1964	65,176	1.39	5,312	12:1
1965	64,506	1.37	4,938	13:1
1966	64,628	1.36	4,590	14:1
1967	64,575	1.35	4,381	15:1
1968	64,461	1.34	4,235	15:1
1970	64,173	1.32	—	—
1971	63,000	1.30	3,687	17:1

Sources: Annual Reports 1952–71 of the Ministry of Health, later the Department of Health and Social Security. Institutions include hospitals vested in the Minister of Health; hospitals under Regional Hospital Boards; Rampton, Moss-side and Broadmoor; in premises not vested in the Minister of Health but deemed to be mental deficiency accommodations; in certified institutions.

residents in 'premises not vested in the Minister of Health but deemed to be mental deficiency accommodations'.

Over a twenty-year period, 1952–71, there has been an 8 per cent increase in the number of patients institutionalized at any point in time[40]. During this same period the general population increased by over 10 per cent (1951–71, 11.4 per cent). Although there were fluctuations in institutional rates over these two decades, with slight increases in the mid-1950s and mid-1960s, the overall rates of institutionalization have remained remarkably constant.

Table 4.4   *Admissions to institutions for the mentally handicapped, 1952–71, England and Wales*

Year	Males	Rates per 100,000 pop.	Female	Rates 100,000 pop.	Total	Rates per 100,000 pop.
1952	1,938	9.2	1,685	7.4	3,623	8.2
1954	1,801	8.4	1,370	5.9	3,171	7.1
1955	1,356	8.2	1,485	6.3	3,214	7.2
1956	1,886	8.7	1,566	6.7	3,452	7.7
1957	1,979	9.1	1,367	5.8	3,346	7.4
1958	2,489	11.4	2,067	8.8	4,556	10.0
1959	2,651	12.0	2,180	9.2	4,831	10.6
1962	4,529	20.2	3,558	14.9	8,087	17.4
1964	4,742	20.9	3,714	15.4	8,456	18.0
1965	4,924	21.5	3,920	16.1	8,849	18.8
1966	5,320	23.1	4,191	17.2	9,511	20.1
1967	5,634	24.4	4,360	17.8	9,994	21.0
1968	5,714	24.6	4,572	18.5	10,286	21.4
1971	6,399	27.0	5,271	21.0	11,670	23.9

Sources: Annual Reports 1952–71 of the Ministry of Health, later the Department of Health and Social Security.

From 1952 to 1959 patterns of institutionalization presented a fairly static picture. There were minimal fluctuations in institutional rates and rates of admission and some indication that waiting lists were decreasing. The pattern for the 1960s was quite different. The institutional rate rose sharply between 1962 and 1963, remained at this level for three years and then returned to the lower level towards the end of the decade. The waiting list continued to grow smaller while admission rates accelerated. This twenty-year period, 1952–71 ended with the same proportion of mentally handicapped in institutions but with admission rates three times higher (23.9 per 100,000 population, compared to 8.2 per 100,000).

However, these data, especially for the 1950s, obscure significant changes. While the admission rates were 8.2 per 100,000 population in the period 1949–51, the specific rates for those between five and fifteen years of age were two to three times higher than those in other age groups. By 1958–60 significant changes had occurred and more in the older groups (fifteen to thirty-five) were being admitted. By 1966 the pattern had shifted again and the trend was reversed. The admission rates doubled and twice as many children under five years of age and considerably more in age group five to ten were being admitted to institutions.

Table 4.5   *Admission rates per 100,000 population to institutions for the mentally handicapped, 1949–66*

Age	1949–51	1958–60	1966
0–4	8.2	9.0	17.4
5–9	14.4	16.4	24.7
10–14	18.0	12.4	18.5
15–19	24.9	29.5	25.7
20–24	8.3	13.2	10.6
25–34	4.8	7.6	5.8
35+	1.9	4.6	2.8
Total	8.2	10.6	20.1

Sources: M. Bone, B. Spain and F. Martin, *Plans and Provisions for the Mentally Handicapped*, Allen and Unwin, 1972, p. 41; Ministry of Health, *Psychiatric Hospitals and Units in England and Wales*, Statistical Report Series no. 4, 1969, p. 79.

At first glance these trends in admissions might suggest that there have in fact been increasing transfers of the caring function from the family to the State. Families would appear to have given over their responsibilities earlier than in the 1950s. These data are incomplete and need to be expanded by examining patient movement. To be admitted to an institution is one thing. A more important question is related to the length of stay.

In 1949 admission to an institution meant long-term care. Bone and her colleagues[41] on the basis of a cohort study, reported that 81 per cent of those admitted in that year were still in institutions after two years and 68 per cent after six years. Analysing it by age, they found that 68 per cent of the patients under five, 86 per cent of those between five and nine and 75 per cent between ten and fifteen were still in institutions after two years. Among those admitted in 1959 the percentage still in institutions after two years had dropped to 51 per cent and to 40 per cent after six years; 47 per cent of those under five; 44 per cent of those between five and nine and 51 per cent of those between ten and fifteen were still institutionalized at the end of two years. In ten years' time there were significant increases in discharges among each age group.

Table 4.6 *Admissions and discharges, institutions for the mentally handicapped, 1964—66*

Admissions (ages)				Discharges (ages)			
Year	Total	0—4	5—9	10—15	Total	0—4	5—9	10—15
1964	10,700	1,002	1,643	1,396	7,510	608	1,176	1,063
1965	10,226	1,040	1,724	1,339	7,802	677	1,292	1,031
1966	10,707	1,074	1,748	1,339	7,707	735	1,370	1,076

Note: These data are for admissions to and discharges from mental subnormality hospitals and units under Regional Hospital Boards. During this period readmissions accounted for 58 per cent of all admissions.

Source: Adapted from Ministry of Health, *Psychiatric Hospitals and Units in England and Wales,* Statistical Report Series no. 4, 1969, pp. 78—9, 98—100.

This trend has continued throughout the 1960s. Readmissions outnumbered first admissions and length of stay was reduced sharply. Between 1964 and 1966, for every 100 admissions there were 70 discharges. This ratio was similar for the age group five to nine, slightly lower for the group nought to four, but much higher for the older children (77 discharged for every 100 admissions). The decade of the 1950s, characterized by little movement, gave way to a relatively dynamic era in institutional care.

The data in Table 4.7, while reporting only on discharges and therefore not comparable to Bone's cohort study, do provide further evidence of this fluidity and help to explain the higher admission rates. The institutions simply were being utilized differently. During the period 1964 to 1966, almost one of every two patients discharged had been institutionalized for less than one month (47 per cent) and six of ten for one month or

Table 4.7 *Discharges from institutions for the mentally handicapped by length of stay, 1964—66 (percentages)*

	3 months or less			6 months or less		
Ages	1964	1965	1966	1964	1965	1966
Under 2	95	97	92	98	100	100
2—4	93	94	92	99	99	98
5—9	87	87	90	95	94	96
10—14	78	80	78	85	88	87
All ages	61	62	64	72	74	85

Source: Adapted from Ministry of Health, *Psychiatric Hospitals and Units in England and Wales,* Statistical Report Series no. 4, 1969, pp. 95—7.

less. This trend has continued into the 1970s where more than half of the total admissions were classified as short-term. While admission rates for children under the age of ten were twice as high as those of the 1950s, their stays were shorter. Nine of every ten children discharged had stayed for three months or less.

There have been other changes over the past twenty years. In 1952 approximately 48 per cent of all in-patients were classified as severely mentally handicapped. By 1970 this group represented over seven of every ten institutional residents (74 per cent). Assuming an estimated prevalence rate of 2.5 per 1,000 population (severe mental handicap) it can be estimated that four of every ten severely handicapped are in institutions. Furthermore, the percentage of severely handicapped in institutions has risen significantly since the 1950s (assuming a similar prevalence rate)[42].

Institutional rates (severely subnormal and subnormal) have remained at the same level over the past twenty years, while rates of admission have tripled. Younger children are more likely to be admitted to institutions

Table 4.8   *Estimates of the percentage of severely mentally handicapped in institutions, 1952—70, England and Wales*

Year	Total of all mentally handicapped institutionalized	Estimated number of severely handicapped institutionalized	Percentage of severely handicapped institutionalized
1952	58,289	28,000	25.4
1959	60,469	37,000	32.4
1962	61,471	39,000	33.6
1965	64,506	43,000	36.4
1970	64,173	47,000	38.5

Notes: (*1*) N. O'Connor and J. Tizard, *The Social Problem of Mental Deficiency*, Pergamon Press, 1954. A 1952 survey found that 48 per cent of residents were classified as idiot or imbecile; J. Leeson, *Demand for Care in Hospitals for the Mentally Subnormal*, Department of Social and Preventive Medicine, University of Manchester, 1962. A 1959 survey found 62 per cent of the residents to be low or medium grade mentally handicapped; surveys carried out from 1962 to 1967 report that severely handicapped represented 64 to 66 per cent of the institutional population: A. Kushlick and G. Cox, 'The ascertained prevalence of mental subnormality in the Wessex Region on 1st July, 1963', *Proceedings of the First International Congress for the Scientific Study of Mental Deficiency*, Montpelier, 1968; M. Bone, B. Spain and F. Martin, *Plans and Provisions for the Mentally Handicapped*, Allen and Unwin, 1972; P. Morris, *Put Away*, Routledge and Kegan Paul, 1969. A 1970 survey found that 74 per cent of residents were severely subnormal. King's Fund, *Census of Mentally Handicapped Patients in Hospital, England and Wales*, Mental Handicap Papers, no. 1, 1972.

(*2*) Percentage based on an estimated prevalence rate of 2.5 per 1,000 population — see Table 4.1.

Table 4.9   *Distribution of the institutional population by age and degree of handicap, 1970, England and Wales*

Age group	Severely subnormal (%)	Subnormal (%)	Total (%)	Age distribution of general population (%)
Under 2	0.09	0.01	0.07	3.20
2—4	0.78	0.21	0.63	4.90
5—9	4.59	0.82	3.60	8.30
10—14	6.88	1.96	5.80	7.40
15—19	8.54	5.22	7.60	6.80
20—24	10.23	7.16	9.40	7.70
25—34	17.27	12.31	15.90	12.40
35—44	14.96	14.47	14.80	11.70
45—54	15.59	18.24	16.30	12.40
55—64	12.86	20.56	14.80	11.90
Over 64	8.21	19.04	11.10	13.30
	(100.00)	(100.00)	(100.00)	(100.00)

Source: King's Fund, *Census of Mentally Handicapped Patients in Hospital, England and Wales*, Mental Handicap Papers no. 1, 1972.

but they tend to remain for short periods. A recent census of the mentally handicapped in institutions estimated that patients under the age of fifteen represent 10 per cent of in-patient population and that severely subnormal children represent 12 per cent of all severely subnormal in-patients. Yet in the general population children under the age of fifteen make up 24 per cent of the total population (1971 Census). It is only in the age group fifteen to nineteen that the percentage of severely subnormal in-patients begins to exceed the expected distribution, indicating that families are likely to keep their severely handicapped children at home, supported by short-term relief, and that they seek longer-term institutional care after their children reached fifteen. Among the less severely handicapped, only 3 per cent of the in-patients are under fifteen years of age and 42 per cent are under forty-five compared to 62 per cent of the general population in that age group. Well over nine of every ten institutionalized children were classified as severely handicapped compared to seven of every ten for all age groups. These figures are slightly lower than those reported by Morris and Bone in the earlier surveys[43]. Admittedly these data are limited, but when correlated with other information they suggest that families are not giving up their responsibility to care for the severely handicapped child.

Although admission rates have increased significantly, it has been estimated that slightly over seven of every ten children and almost one of every two adults who are severely handicapped are living with their families[44]. Are the severely handicapped in institutions different from those living in the community? Among the younger group there are clear differences. While most severely handicapped children have considerable incapacities (80 per cent), children in institutions were even more likely to be non-ambulant, severely incontinent, and have behaviour problems requiring constant supervision. However, it should be emphasized that these are relative differences. Long-term or permanent institutionalization among children is not the norm. Statistically, longer-term transfer of the caring function is more likely to occur after the child is fifteen years of age and when a child is placed, he is usually considerably handicapped. Morris reported that in 1964 among the younger institutional population 10 per cent had physical deformities, 12 per cent were totally paralysed, 10 per cent were partially paralysed, 11 per cent 'suffered from mutism', 7 per cent had motor handicaps, and 6 per cent had severe speech defects[45].

Table 4.10   *Institutional and non-institutional severely mentally handi-capped by age and incapacity*

Incapacity	0—14 years		15 years and over	
	Home	Institution	Home	Institution
Non-ambulant	21.4	30.6	4.5	7.5
Behaviour difficulties requiring constant supervision	9.8	24.4	4.4	16.3
Severely incontinent	10.2	18.3	2.4	7.3
Needing assistance in feeding, washing and dressing	32.4	18.2	13.0	17.3
No physical handicap or severe behaviour difficulties	26.2	8.5	75.7	51.6
	(100.0)	(100.0)	(100.0)	(100.0)

Source: Adapted from DHSS, *Better Services for the Mentally Handicapped*, Cmnd 4683, HMSO, 1972.

Still, the major contributing factor appeared to be problems associated with behaviour or management. A second reason was either some family crisis or the illness or death of the person providing care[46]. Yet Tizard and Grad found in their earlier study 'in spite of the obvious hardships which many families had to bear in caring for a mentally handicapped child at home, the proportion who wished for institutional care was small[47]. If this is the case and families do not want to relinquish the caring function, it becomes critical to assess the health and welfare resources that are available to support them.

Community services

Even before the passage of the 1959 Mental Health Act the slow but gradual reorientation to community care had begun. The Wood Committee in 1929 strongly urged the government to develop community-based services for the mentally handicapped. In 1954—55, local authorities had expended more than £2 million on community mental health services. By 1957—58 expenditure amounted to £3.5 million, and in 1958—59, £4 million[48]. The Royal Commission on Mental Illness and Mental Deficiency in their report of 1957 strongly urged that hospitals should be used primarily for 'helpless patients in the severely subnormal group who needed continual nursing if proper care cannot be provided at home . . . in-patient training for severely subnormal and psychopathic patients if such training requires individual psychiatric supervision[49]. These recommendations were accepted and under the 1959 Act local authorities were to provide a full range of community services for the mentally handicapped. This position was reaffirmed in 1968 in the Report of the Committee on Local Authority and Allied Personal Social Services[50] and in 1971 by the Department of Health and Social Security[51]. The new emphasis was to be on community based residential accommodations, training centres, sheltered workshops and social support services.

Table 4.11   *Number of mentally handicapped known to local authorities, 1947—70, England and Wales*

Year	Number	Rates/1,000 population	Year	Number	Rates/1,000 population
1947	49,902	1.16	1961	81,885	1.78
1948	50,511	1.17	1962	83,984	1.81
1949	51,716	1.19	1963	85,628	1.84
1950	52,390	1.20	1964	87,743	1.87
1951	53,899	1.23	1965	90,384	1.92
1952	59,830	1.36	1966	93,486	1.97
1953	58,889	1.33	1967	97,476	2.04
1954	61,037	1.37	1968	99,820	2.07
1955	62,729	1.40	1969	102,586	2.13
1956	63,551	1.41	1970	104,140	2.15
1957	63,327	1.40			
1959	62,546	1.37			

Note: *1947—59* Includes those 'under guardianship or notified' and those under 'statutory supervision'.

1961—70 Includes those 'receiving Mental Health Services provided by Local Health Authorities'.

Sources: Annual Reports 1952—71 of the Ministry of Health, later the Department of Health and Social Security.

In 1947 almost 50,000 mentally handicapped persons were known to local authorities. Of these 90 per cent were in the category 'under statutory supervision' and the remainder (5,373) under 'guardianship or notified'. By 1959, the year the Mental Health Act was passed, the number known had increased by 27 per cent, showing an average annual increase of slightly more than 2 per cent. However, the number under 'guardianship and notification' shrank to slightly over 2,000 people or 3 per cent of the total. In part this was due to a conscious policy of voluntary supervision for which no statistics are available.

The 1959 Act removed the statutory supervision requirement and following this, statistics were reported on the numbers 'receiving services from local health authorities'. A more meaningful and operational description of this new category is probably one which refers to people known by the local authorities. Two years later almost 82,000 mentally handicapped children and adults were known to the new Mental Health Authorities, an increase over 1959 of 31 per cent. By 1970 the number grew to more than 104,000, double the numbers receiving services in 1947.

These data included all categories of mental handicap and it was only in 1963 that specific data on the severely handicapped began to be reported. From 1963 to 1970 the ratio of severely handicapped to mildly handicapped under local authority care remained at one to one. During this eight-year period there was an increase of 23 per cent in the numbers of the severely handicapped receiving care (compared to 21 per cent for all handicapped). If these data are examined more closely, it becomes clear that priority was given to children over adults (increases of 36 per cent and 15 per cent respectively). If the prevalence rates of the 1960s are reason-

Table 4.12   *Number of severely mentally handicapped under local authority care, 1963—70, England and Wales*

	0–15		Over 15		Total	
Year	Number	Rates/ 1,000	Number	Rates/ 1,000	Number	Rates/ 1,000
1963	16,908	1.57	27,309	0.76	44,217	0.95
1964	17,485	1.61	28,062	0.78	45,547	0.97
1965	18,148	1.65	28,618	0.79	46,766	0.99
1966	19,219	1.73	29,156	0.80	48,375	1.02
1967	20,693	1.85	30,041	0.82	50,734	1.06
1968	21,623	1.92	30,289	0.82	51,912	1.08
1969	22,491	1.98	30,842	0.84	53,333	1.11
1970	23,066	2.01	31,305	0.84	54,371	1.12

Note: Rates per 1,000 are specific to the two age categories.

Source: DHSS, *Health and Personal Social Service Statistics for England*, HMSO, 1973, p. 134.

ably accurate (3.6 per 1,000 for the population under fifteen years of age and 2.5 per 1,000 for all age groups) 45 per cent of all the severely handicapped and 56 per cent of severely handicapped children were under local authority care in 1970, compared to 38 per cent and 44 per cent in 1963. These years can be characterized as a period of considerable casefinding and outreach, a necessary component for an effective community care system. Undoubtedly these increases were affected by a more favourable reaction on the part of the general public and families with handicapped children following the passage of the 1959 Act. Expectations were stimulated and demand for service increased.

Specific services for the severely mentally handicapped also showed relative growth. In 1963, 295 severely handicapped children were in residential care (occupying 82 per cent of the total number of places for mentally handicapped children) and 404 adults (42 per cent of the total adult places). By 1970, 1,404 severely handicapped children and 2,044 adults were in such accommodation, representing increases of 376 per cent and 600 per cent respectively. However, when age is controlled children appeared to receive higher priority over this period with residential care rates consistently twice as high as those for the older group.

Table 4.13 *Number of severely mentally handicapped in residential care, 1963—70, England and Wales*

Year	0—15 Number	0—15 Rate/ 100,000	Over 15 Number	Over 15 Rate/ 100,000	Total Number	Total Rate/ 100,000
1963	295	2.7	404	1.1	699	1.5
1964	502	4.6	598	1.7	1,100	2.3
1965	574	5.2	885	2.4	1,459	3.1
1966	837	7.5	1,222	3.4	2,059	4.3
1967	980	8.8	1,378	3.8	2,358	4.9
1968	1,116	9.9	1,614	4.4	2,730	5.7
1969	1,262	11.1	1,913	5.2	3,175	6.6
1970	1,404	12.2	2,044	5.4	3,448	7.1

Note: Rates per 100,000 are specific to the two age categories.

Source: DHSS, *Health and Personal Social Service Statistics for England*, HMSO, 1973, p. 135.

From 1963 to 1970, the number of children enrolled in junior training centres had increased by 59 per cent (from 14,000 to 22,000) and the number of adults in training centres doubled (from 13,000 to 26,000). During this period, eight of every ten children and two of every three adults in these centres were classified as severely handicapped. As with residential care, higher priority appears to have been given to children.

Table 4.14   *Number of severely mentally handicapped in training centres, 1963—70, England and Wales*

Year	0–15		Over 15		Total	
	Number	Rates/ 100,000	Number	Rates/ 100,000	Number	Rates/ 100,000
1963	11,625	108	8,917	25	20,542	44
1964	12,419	114	10,053	28	22,472	48
1965	13,228	120	11,136	31	24,364	52
1966	13,994	126	12,062	33	26,056	55
1967	15,076	135	13,288	36	28,364	59
1968	16,030	142	14,024	38	30,054	63
1969	16,797	145	14,803	40	31,600	65
1970	17,598	153	15,773	43	33,371	69

Note: Rates per 100,000 are specific to the two age categories.

Source: DHSS, *Health and Personal Social Service Statistics for England*, HMSO, 1973, p. 134.

Utilization rates were three-and-a-half to four times higher for the younger age group[52].

In 1961 there were 1,128 social workers employed in mental health work by local authorities. The next eight years saw steady annual growth and by 1969 they numbered 1,808 an increase of 60 per cent. In the year immediately preceding the implementation of the Mental Health Act, expenditure on community mental health services represented slightly over 6 per cent of all local authority health expenditures and by 1969, this proportion had been increased to 13 per cent[53].

Given these new commitments to community care and increased efforts to sensitize professionals to provide greater support to families choosing to care for the mentally handicapped, quick results were hoped for. A number of studies were carried out during this period to evaluate its impact[54]. A major focus of this research was the level of support provided by various health and social service personnel. Their findings were discouraging.

Forty-four per cent of the mothers in Hewitt's survey and 35 per cent of those in Bayley's study reported that they did not find their general practitioners to be very supportive. Moncrieff in her 1963 study, soon after the passage of the 1959 Act, found that 89 per cent of the families had been visited by a local authority social worker at least once over the previous five years. Of those visited, 8 per cent were hostile to the social workers, 30 per cent indifferent, 38 per cent thought the social worker to be pleasant but of no particular help, 15 per cent felt the social worker to be sympathetic and understanding, and only 9 per cent reported that they had been a practical help. She concluded that:

Table 4.15   *Number of severely mentally handicapped boarding out or in private homes at local authority expense, 1963—70, England and Wales*

Year	0—15		Over 15		Total	
	Number	Rate/ 100,000	Number	Rate/ 100,000	Number	Rate/ 100,000
1963	70	0.64	214	0.59	284	0.61
1964	66	0.61	226	0.63	292	0.62
1965	60	0.55	209	0.58	269	0.57
1966	58	0.52	207	0.57	265	0.56
1967	49	0.44	234	0.64	283	0.59
1968	50	0.44	245	0.67	295	0.61
1969	45	0.39	293	0.79	338	0.70
1970	70	0.61	257	0.69	304	0.63

Note: Rates per 100,000 are specific to the two age categories.

Source: DHSS, *Health and Personal Social Service Statistics for England*, HMSO, 1973, p. 135.

The overall picture of the work of MWOs [Mental Welfare Officers] . . . suggests that the help given to the families of the subnormal is insufficiently related to their needs. The lack of flexibility seems to result from adherence to administrative procedures. The focus is on the subnormal person himself, and his family surroundings, although essential to his welfare, are too often not taken into account. The narrowness of this approach is serious because social workers could provide the channel by which the needs for improvements in practical services are made known. . . .

Unfortunately, social work with the mentally handicapped has for many years been regarded as low in status compared with other branches of the profession such as child care and probation. This may have been partly . . . because investment in the subnormal unlike the deprived child has been regarded as wasted[55].

Hewitt, in her study a few years later, found that almost eight of every ten families had had no contact with local authority social workers, 14 per cent had two or less visits in a year, and 8 per cent three or more. It should be noted that statutory visiting was no longer required by this time. While contact with social workers from official agencies was limited, 83 per cent of the families had had some contact with social workers, primarily from the voluntary sector. Eighteen per cent regarded the visiting with indifference, 23 per cent reported they would give a qualified welcome to social work visits and 52 per cent without reservation. Most significantly, seven of ten mothers stated they would not want to be visited more often. Why?

A difficulty arises if the kind of help which the family needs cannot be supplied by the worker, however resourceful he or she may be. . . . In this situation of scarce and inadequate provision, which applied particularly to the mentally handicapped who also have physical handicaps, the caseworker is in a very difficult position[56].

Bayley's study was carried out in 1968, almost a decade after the passage of the Mental Health Act. He found that all of the handicapped children, but only 44 per cent of the adults had been visited by local authority social workers during the twenty months preceding his survey period. Slightly over half (51 per cent) of the mothers who had had a contact felt the social worker provided little or no help, 38 per cent some help and 19 per cent significant help.

There appeared to be a general uncertainty among the mental welfare officers about the sort of service they should be trying to offer to the sub-normals and their families, let alone how to offer it. . . . It may be that the psychodynamic bias of social workers and social work training does not make them sufficiently aware of the mundane 'slog' of caring for the subnormal. But, fundamentally, I am convinced that the social work help which was offered was simply irrelevant[57].

While these observations on the potential contribution of social workers are discouraging, some shifts, as small as they might be, are encouraging. The earliest study reported that 76 per cent of the families were either hostile or indifferent to social workers or felt them to be of no help. The latest study showed that 56 per cent of the families felt the same.

Families who had contact with health visitors were quite positive to these contacts but this service was limited to families with children under five years of age. In all these studies there is mention of only one family receiving home help services[58]. In Hunt's national survey of the Home Help Service there is no specific mention of services being utilized by families with mentally handicapped members[59]. Although it would be simplistic to equate 'visits' with family support, it can be assumed that in the absence of contact there is no support by the official agencies.

A reorganization of the Personal Social Services occurred in 1970. The basis for this reorganization, the Seebohm Report, recommended that the new social service departments 'take responsibility for the care of mentally subnormal children and their families', and that these departments 'will need to see themselves not as a self-contained unit but as a part of a network of services within the community'[60]. Social workers in these new departments, unlike their predecessors, would have some degree of control over a number of critical resources, for example, the domiciliary services, aids and adaptations, and residential care places. The Department of Health and Social Security reaffirmed this position in 1971. 'The person best placed to act as coordinator is likely to be the social worker'[61]. However, at this time there is little systematic data available that attempts to assess the impact of these developments[62].

Discussion

Before the Second World War, little attention was paid to families with mentally handicapped members or to the concept of community care. Policy implicitly favoured segregation of the handicapped in long-term care institutions. It was strongly believed that this approach was in the best interest of the individual concerned and was the most effective way to protect society. Since 1946 there has been a marked shift in policy. The National Health Service Act, 1946, and the National Assistance Act, 1948, attempted to bring about some rationality, balance and accountability into the issue of appropriate care for the handicapped. In 1959 the State formally recognized that the majority of the mentally handicapped were living with their families; that institutionalization was not necessarily the most desirable form of care and that families could benefit from a network of social support services. This principle was reaffirmed by the Chronically Sick and Disabled Persons Act, 1970, the Local Authority Social Services Act, 1970, in so far as this legislation was based on the Report of the Seebohm Committee, the Education Act, 1971, and the White Paper, *Better Services for the Mentally Handicapped*, 1971. The new emphasis was to be on the appropriate balance of community and institutional services.

These developments are, of course, the explicit policies of the State. The more critical issue is their implementation and effect. If emphasis is now on services to support the family, is institutionalization — where the State takes over from the family — decreasing? Are families receiving support from the State and thus becoming more capable of functioning as the primary care unit?

The data on institutional care are inconclusive. Rates of institutionalization in the large facilities have remained remarkably constant since 1952 and increases in numbers in institutions have been less than increases in the population. However, these data are incomplete. If those in local authority residential care accommodation are added to the above, the overall institutional rate in 1970 would have been closer to 1.43 per 1,000 population, a rate that was higher than that in 1952. Community residential care, considered more desirable than care in the segregated large hospital institution, is still institutional care. Families may have more contact with the mentally handicapped residents, the environment may be more 'normal', but in principle the State has still substituted for the family and there has been a transfer of the caring function. A significant trend over the past ten years is the increased rates of admission, accompanied by higher discharge rates. The institutions are being used more for short-term stays. A growing number of families appear to transfer the caring function, but only on a temporary basis. Current policy, however, does not seem to be emphasizing a decrease in institutional care but actually increased levels of provision are being planned. The Department of Health and Social Security has estimated that a desirable level would be 1.58 per 1,000 (0.88 per 1,000 in long-term care institutions and 0.69 per 1,000 in residential care accommodation)[63], a rate that is considerably higher than the present rate. The concern now is to shift the locus of the 'institutional' care.

Patterns in community care are less conclusive. Following the Mental Health Act, 1959, services for the mentally handicapped began to expand. By 1970, 56 per cent of the estimated number of severely handicapped children and 38 per cent of the severely handicapped adults were under the care of the local authority. While this shows significant improvement over 1963, the percentage is unreasonably low if it can be assumed that local authorities at least are aware of those families caring for the severely mentally handicapped. The issue is not the provision of services to all these families. Many do not want or need ongoing care or support. The term 'under care' also includes those who are known to the local authority and in turn know what services are available. Three per cent of the severely handicapped were in residential care accommodation; 28 per cent in special schools or training centres and less than 0.25 per cent boarded out in private homes. Priority appears to have been given to children, but this has to be interpreted realistically in light of an extremely low level of provision for the adult group.

Table 4.16   *Utilization rates of various community services by the severely mentally handicapped, 1970*

	Children		*Adults*		*Total*	
Type of care	Utiliza-tion	Penetra-tion (%)	Utiliza-tion	Penetra-tion (%)	Utiliza-tion	Penetra-tion (%)
Under care — L.A.	2.01	56.0	0.84	38.0	1.12	45.0
Residential care	0.12	3.3	0.05	2.2	0.07	3.0
Training centres/ spec. schools	1.53	42.0	0.43	19.0	0.69	28.0
Boarding out	0.006	0.2	0.007	0.3	0.006	0.25

Note: Penetration is used in the sense of uptake of services by the estimated target groups. In calculating this penetration, the following prevalence rates of severely mentally handicapped were utilized: 3.6 per 1,000 for the age group 0—15; 2.2 per 1,000 for those over fifteen years of age; and 2.5 per 1,000 for the total population.

Day care or education for children under the age of five was miniscule and seven times as many places are needed to meet official targets. Even with the long standing priority given to the expansion of special schools for children there was an estimated 29 per cent deficit in the number of places. Adult places in occupation and training centres need to be doubled. While the State has highlighted the need for social work services, domiciliary services (e.g. home helps, home nursing) and practical assistance (e.g. laundry service, holidays, sitters, etc.) few systematic data related to the question of adequacy are available and the Department of Health and Social Security has concluded that '. . . quantitative targets cannot be set . . . but some allowance must be made for their cost in any forecast of rate of progress in local authority services for the mentally handicapped'[64]. For families with children under five years, ineligible for the special schools, it is these services together with day care that may make a difference. As was shown earlier, there are an estimated 16,000 severely mentally handicapped children in this age group, 11,000 of whom are living with their families.

To sum up, then, despite the fact that demand has increased steadily over the past fifteen years and the indications are that it will probably continue growing, it is extremely difficult to relate these trends to the issue of family responsibility. Estimated shortages are considerable and even if demand were to increase sharply over the next decade, any conclusions would have to be tentative. For example, if the State were to reach its institutional target of 1.58 places per 1,000 population (both large institutions and community residential care), this would mean an increase of 15 per cent over present rates. If the proposed target for children were reached, 23 per cent more children would be institutionalized[65]. And yet, how meaningful is this rate and what inferences could be drawn if it were to be exceeded? For example, Tizard earlier suggested a rate of 25 per 1,000[66] and Page and Jones estimated the need for 19.8 per 1,000[67]. The concept of need and standards is crucial to this enquiry and will be dealt with in the next chapter. As with the elderly the State seems to have established priorities that emphasize its residual approach to social welfare. Services are more likely to be available to the mentally handicapped when their families are unable or unwilling to provide care. Comparable levels of provision are not available to families who wish to retain the primary caring function but could benefit from support services.

In spite of the fact that support services are grossly inadequate, it seems that most families do want to maintain their mentally handicapped children for as long as possible, and this is the key. The issue is not one form of care over the other, institutional care rather than non-institutional care or vice versa. Tizard states the policy issue clearly:

In principle, at least, parents of the mentally handicapped have the choice whether to keep a grossly handicapped child at home or to place him in institutional care. It is right that they should have this choice, even though it is one which they must find it very difficult to exercise. . . . Now some experts on mental subnormality believe that parents should always strive to keep a handicapped child at home, irrespective of the family's circumstances. There are others who usually advise hospital care. . . . It is only when both the domiciliary services and the institutional services are as good as we can make them that the choice can remain open . . . what prevents people from being able to make a rational choice between the alternatives, is the inadequacy of the services[68].

References

1. Impairment and handicapped as used by A. Harris, *Handicapped and Impaired in Great Britain*, OPCS, Social Survey Division, HMSO, 1971, p. 2.

2. Age Concern, *The Attitudes of the Retired and the Elderly*, Manifesto Series, no. 32, Research Report, London, October 1974.

3. K. Jones, *Mental Health and Social Policy: 1845–1959*, Routledge and Kegan Paul, 1967, p. 45.

4. There were of course exceptions such as the Elementary Education Act of 1899, which allowed education authorities to establish special schools or classes for all defectives of school age, to board them near these schools or to provide transportation for them. While this approach would appear to encourage a form of community care, the outcome was exactly the opposite. Again, as with so many other forms of social legislation, the Act was permissive and not compulsory.

5. C. P. Lapage, *Feeble-mindedness in Children of School Age* (1920) cited in K. Jones, op. cit. (ref. 3), p. 48.

6. *Report of the Royal Commission on the Poor Laws and Relief of Distress*, Cd 4499, Vol. III, Chapter 6, 1909, p. 234.

7. K. Jones, op. cit. (ref. 3), pp. 58, 76, 84.

8. Ibid., pp. 43, 54, 65.

9. Ibid., p. 67.

10. P. Townsend in P. Morris, *Put Away*, Routledge and Kegan Paul, 1969, Foreword, pp. xiii–xix.

11. K. Jones, op. cit. (ref. 3), p. 146.

12. See J. Tizard, 'Epidemiology of mental retardation: implications for research on malnutrition', in *Early Malnutrition and Mental Development*, eds, J. Cravioto, L. Hambraeus and B. Vahlquist, Symposia of the Swedish Nutrition Foundation, no. 12, Uppsala, Almquist and Wiksell, 1974. Tizard's contribution provides an excellent review of significant epidemiological studies carried out in the United Kingdom.

13. DHSS, *Better Services for the Mentally Handicapped*, Cmnd 4683, HMSO, 1971.

14. J. Tizard, 'Implications for services of recent social research in mental retardation', in *The Mentally Subnormal*, eds, M. Adams and H. Lovejoy, Heinemann Medical Books, 1972, p. 272.

15. Ibid., p. 273.

16. *Better Services for the Mentally Handicapped*, op. cit. (ref. 13), pp. 28, 66–7.

17. J. Tizard, op. cit. (ref. 14), p. 273.

18. J. Tizard, op. cit. (ref. 12), pp. 37–8.

19. See for example: J. Tizard and J. Grad. *The Mentally Handicapped and their Families: A Social Survey*, Oxford University Press, 1961; J. Moncrieff, *Mental Subnormality in London: A Survey of Community Care*, PEP, 1966; A. Kushlick, (*a*) 'The prevalence of recognized mental subnormality of IQ under 50 among children in the south of England with reference to the demand for places for residential care', *Proceedings of the International Copenhagen Congress on the Scientific Study of Mental Retardation*, August 1964, and (*b*) 'Social problems of mental subnormality', in *Foundations of Child Psychiatry*, Pergamon Press, 1968; M. Bayley, *Mental Handicap and Community Care*, Routledge and Kegan Paul, 1973.

20. *Better Services for the Mentally Handicapped*, op. cit. (ref. 13), p. 5.

21. M. Bone, B. Spain and F. M. Martin, *Plans and Provisions for the Mentally Handicapped*, National Institute for Social Work Training Series no. 23, Allen and Unwin, 1972.

22. P. Cohen, 'The impact of the handicapped child on the family', *Social Casework*, 43, no. 3, 1962, 137–42.

23. E. Reid, 'Helping parents of handicapped children', *Children*, Jan./Feb. 1958, pp. 15–19.

24. K. Holt, 'The home care of the severely retarded child', *Pediatrics*, October 1958, pp. 746–55.

25. C. Fowle, 'The effect of the severely mentally retarded child on his family', *American Journal of Mental Deficiency*, 73, 1968, 468–73.

26. See for example S. Hewitt, *The Family and the Handicapped Child*, Allen and Unwin, 1972.

27. This is the same conclusion drawn by Shanas in her suggestion that families are not neglecting their elderly relatives. Those that do are a minority and it is this small number who come into contact with the social agencies. This was discussed in Ch. 2. E. Shanas, 'The unmarried old person in the United States: living arrangements and care in illness, myth or fact', paper prepared for the International Social Service Research Seminar in Gerontology, Markaryd, Sweden, August 1963.

28. K. Holt, op. cit. (ref. 24).

29. J. Tizard and J. Grad, op. cit. (ref. 19), pp. 78ff.

30. See for example F. Schonell and B. Watts, 'A first survey of the effects of a subnormal child on the family unit', *American Journal of Mental Deficiency*, 61, 1956, 210–19; J. Kershaw, 'The handicapped child and his family', *Public Health*, 80, 1965, 18–26; J. Peck and W. Stephens, 'A study of the relationships between the attitudes and

behaviour of parents and that of their mentally defective child',
American Journal of Mental Deficiency, 64, 1960, 839.

31. J. Kershaw, op. cit. (ref. 30).

32. K. Holt, op. cit. (ref. 24).

33. See: J. Tizard and J. Grad, op. cit. (ref. 19); K. Holt, op. cit. (ref. 24);
    J. Kershaw, op. cit. (ref. 30).

34. Statistics at best only provide a quantitative picture. The author was
    deeply impressed by the insights recorded by Bayley and Hewitt in
    their studies. M. Bayley, op. cit. (ref. 19), Ch. 15, 'The daily grind';
    S. Hewitt, op. cit. (ref. 26), Ch. 3, 'Practical aspects of day-to-day living'.

35. S. Hewitt, op. cit. (ref. 26), p. 70.

36. J. Tizard and J. Grad, op. cit. (ref. 19).

37. C. Fowle, op. cit. (ref. 25).

38. See for example, K. Holt, op. cit. (ref. 24); F. Schonell and B. Watts,
    op. cit. (ref. 30).

39. See M. Bone, *et al.* op. cit. (ref. 21), pp. 32–6 for a detailed
    discussion of this problem.

40. Unfortunately, reports following 1971 do not include data for
    England and Wales but only for England.

41. M. Bone, *et al.*, op. cit. (ref. 21), p. 111.

42. It is possible that the prevalence rate of 2.5 per 1,000 was not as high
    given higher mortality rates in earlier periods.

43. P. Morris, op. cit. (ref. 10), p. 61; M. Bone, *et al.*, op. cit. (ref. 21),
    p. 61.

44. See *Better Services for the Mentally Handicapped*, op. cit. (ref. 13),
    Table 1, p. 6.

45. P. Morris, op. cit. (ref. 10), p. 71.

46. J. Tizard and J. Grad, op. cit. (ref. 19), found behaviour and manage-
    ment problems to be the primary reason in 51 per cent of the families
    studied; M. Bone *et al.*, op. cit. (ref. 21), 50 per cent; and M. Bayley,
    op. cit. (ref. 19), 46 per cent.

47. J. Tizard, op. cit. (ref. 14), p. 284.

48. K. Jones, op. cit. (ref. 3), p. 187.

49. *Report of the Royal Commission on the Law Relating to Mental
    Illness and Mental Deficiency*, 1954–57, Cmnd 169, 1957.

50. *Report of the Committee on Local Authority and Allied Personal
    Services*, Cmnd 3703, HMSO, 1968, Ch. 11.

51. *Better Services for the Mentally Handicapped*. op. cit. (ref. 13).

52. *Health and Personal Social Services Statistics for England*, HMSO, 1973, p. 134.

53. Various annual reports of the Ministry of Health, later the Department of Health and Social Security.

54. For example see J. Moncrieff, op. cit. (ref. 19), who carried out a follow-up survey of the earlier work of J. Tizard and J. Grad, op. cit. (ref. 19), S. Hewitt, op. cit. (ref. 26), M. Bayley, op. cit. (ref. 19) and the extensive work of A. Kushlick (ref. 19).

55. J. Moncrieff, op. cit. (ref. 19), pp. 58, 74—5.

56. S. Hewitt, op. cit. (ref. 26), pp. 166—70.

57. M. Bayley, op. cit. (ref. 19), pp. 301, 307.

58. Ibid., p. 324.

59. A. Hunt, GSS, *The Home Help Service in England and Wales*, HMSO, 1970. This does not mean that families with mentally handicapped are not receiving this service. However, if they are, their numbers were not large enough to merit identification.

60. *Report of the Committee on Local Authority and Allied Personal Social Services.* op. cit. (ref. 50), paras 363, 478.

61. *Better Services for the Mentally Handicapped*, op. cit. (ref. 13), para. 141.

62. As part of this study, the author in 1974 spent a number of weeks with various local authorities, interviewing almost 100 local authority staff. Since the observations were not based on a representative sample the findings cannot be treated as a true representation of current practice. They are, however, dealt with extensively in the following chapters.

63. *Better Services for the Mentally Handicapped*, op. cit. (ref. 13), extrapolated from Table 5, p. 42.

64. Ibid., para. 209.

65. Ibid., Table 5.

66. J. Tizard, *Community Services for the Mentally Handicapped*, Oxford University Press, 1964.

67. D. Page and K. Jones, *Health and Welfare Services in Britain in 1975*, Cambridge University Press, 1966.

68. J. Tizard, *The Integration of the Handicapped in Society*, The Sixth Bartholomew Lecture delivered at the University of Keele, 4 February 1966, Occasional Papers in Social and Economic Administration, no. 1, London, Edutext Publications, 1966.

5 The family and the State: qualitative and quantitative aspects of a caring function

The focus in the preceding chapters has been on the needs and characteristics of two groups of handicapped persons; the contributions that families make in the caring function as well as the demands this care involves; and the ways in which the State has organized itself to provide assistance. Central to the discussion and the statistics are the questions raised earlier dealing with the nature of the relationship between the family and the State and the complex issue of appropriate areas of responsibility. Up to this point the emphasis has been description, and yet these issues must eventually lead to a discussion of what various social policy instruments might do, or further, what they should be attempting to accomplish: their purpose and the purpose of State intervention.

For over thirty years, there has been little disagreement that the State should function as a primary social institution in society to protect and promote the general welfare of its members. During and after the Second World War the State has operated on the explicit assumption that it has the responsibility to ensure that basic needs will be met, needs related to income, employment, education and physical and social wellbeing. While the principle has been viewed as bipartisan and upheld by successive governments, the issues of what policies best serve the goal of promoting welfare and how the State should actually go about achieving it have been the subject of continuous debate. The arguments have been concerned with a number of basic questions. Are benefits to be provided as of right or are they to be made available only to individuals or families when they meet various eligibility criteria? Should the State attempt to strengthen family life or should it wait until the individual or family is not longer capable of managing on its own? Should benefits be provided to the total population or to specific target groups[1]? Furthermore, should the State restrict its activity to guaranteeing a minimum level of welfare or should it go beyond this by developing mechanisms that seek to improve and promote the quality of social life[2]? Finally, should the State function as the sole provider of social welfare services, the primary provider, or should it share these responsibilities with other institutions[3]?

Although those involved in the debate may identify themselves on either side of these ideological positions, and specific policy proposals will have a foundation in strongly held beliefs, more often than not the policies are shaped by economic factors and practical needs. For these reasons, policies are likely to emerge from compromise and negotiation. For example, the National Insurance Act, 1946, affirmed the principle of universal coverage and benefits as of right. This was later supplemented by the National Assistance Act, 1948, which allowed the Government to provide assistance on an individual basis to those who could meet the requirements of a means test. The National Health Service Act, 1946, and the Education Act, 1944, clearly established the State as the primary provider of medical care and educational services but both allowed the private sector to continue on a fee-for-service basis.

Whereas the earlier debates of the postwar period emphasized ideological differences, by the 1960s the focus appears to have shifted from ends to means, from purposes to specific programmatic intervention. Marshall has suggested that a consensus on these fundamental differences apparently had been reached.

There is little difference of opinion as to the services that must be provided, and it is generally agreed that whoever provides them, the overall responsibility for the welfare of the citizens must remain with the State ... the issues at stake in the sixties turned out to be less concerned with social ideology than with social engineering[4].

However, if this consensus did exist, it now seems to be breaking down. Once again, the fundamental questions concerning the role and purpose of the State are being raised. The issues of increased nationalization of industry, the existence of private hospital beds and private medical practice within the NHS, and the status of private schools, once again are in the forefront of policy debate. Renewed demands for cutbacks in public expenditure, reminiscent of the arguments in the 1950s, have been accompanied by government pressure on local authorities to 'limit their plans only to what is necessary'.

Interestingly enough, this is now the position of the Labour Government while earlier it was the position of the Conservatives. It might be concluded that the consensus of the 1960s either did not exist but that fundamental differences were viewed as relatively unimportant in an expansionary period, or that the consensus was held together by a tenuous bond that only began to come apart when the economic situation was reversed.

This pattern over the past twenty-five years would suggest that ideological disagreements have a tendency to become more important in times of economic crisis, and that ideology is more than the system of beliefs that shapes a particular approach to achieving some desired goals. It is often used to defend or attack existing or proposed courses of action. Equally it is unlikely that these fundamental differences will be resolved, although if the past can be used to predict the future, they will become less important when the economic crisis passes. Unfortunately such debates have a tendency to falter on the definitional ambiguities associated with such concepts as 'the general welfare' and 'quality of life'. While they are constantly being used they are rarely operationalized and often obscure the critical issue of specific State responsibilities. When is it appropriate for the State to involve itself in the provision of social care, in what circumstances and in what ways?

On a theoretical level, there seems to be widespread agreement that the

State has both the right and the responsibility to step in when an individual can no longer meet his own needs or when he does not have other resources to rely on. The isolated elderly person, living alone, infirm or handicapped, needing considerable care and supervision, can be transferred to a hospital or a residential home for his own wellbeing. Children who are neglected or in danger of physical abuse can be removed from their families. The emphasis is on protecting the individual who might harm himself or others or be harmed[5].

The State has also assumed some degree of responsibility in situations not as extreme as the above, where individuals or families are unable to cope adequately. Intervention usually takes place after a crisis or breakdown, and although the State 'substitutes' for certain functions, it is partial rather than complete. The State's role is viewed as marginal and primarily concerned with a small proportion of the population – those who are unable or unwilling to meet their own needs through the normal mechanisms of the market[6].

Underlying both forms of intervention is the State's apparent reluctance to interfere with the family's rights and responsibilities and a traditional concern for privacy and self-determination. There is, still, a clear policy in those situations in which an elderly person or a handicapped child either has no family or the family is unwilling or unable to provide the needed care.

But the elderly and handicapped children of concern to this study are not without resources, and relatively few are in danger of being neglected or abused. They are living with their families, and the weight of evidence suggests that most families are willing to carry the major caring function. By definition they are excluded from the above two categories, those without families and those living with families who are unable to cope adequately and are experiencing severe problems in social functioning. There is no need for a substitute family and furthermore the existing family can be seen as functioning reasonably well or at least managing. What responsibility does the State carry in these situations?

Almost twenty years ago the State implicitly recognized the need to provide supportive services to families in the Mental Health Act, 1959, with its emphasis on community care. A year later this was more explicitly stated in the Ingleby Report on Children and Youth.

The State's principle duty is to assist the family in carrying out its proper functions. This should be done in the first instance by the provision of facilities such as housing, health services and education. Some families will need greater and more specialized help through the welfare services, but such help should always be directed towards building up the responsibility of the parents whenever this is possible[7].

This expression of the principle of State responsibility to assist the family, to strengthen and support its capability to provide social care, is a recent development. The legitimate concern on the part of the State not to interfere unnecessarily, not to take over from the family can, however, prove counterproductive to the development of these necessary services. The dividing line is a fine one that requires close examination.

One possible way is to go beyond statements of general welfare and quality of life and identify a more measurable construct. One that is beginning to gain some currency is that of a caring society and the caring State[8]. The notion is deceptively simple and carries the connotation of being 'interested' in the wellbeing of someone. How caring is the State to families caring for the elderly and mentally handicapped? What are its dimensions and can it be measured?

Dimensions of a caring society: choice, support and shared responsibility

Chapter 4 concluded with the statement that families with mentally handicapped children should have the choice either to continue caring for the child at home or to place him in an institution. The same can be said of those families providing care to elderly parents and grandparents. Choice, of course, is not a simple concept and has to be examined closely. In suggesting that families should have such a choice, this in no way implies that either course is equally desirable in all cases or that both serve the same function.

To put this back into the specifics of this study, in 1971 there were 1,200,000 elderly living with their children and 38 per cent or 450,000 of these elderly persons were over seventy-four years of age. Over 250,000 of the elderly living with their children were handicapped, and of these, more than 50,000 were severely handicapped. Approximately 30,000 severely mentally handicapped children (70 per cent of the total) were living with their parents. In so far as they are providing care, it might be argued that they chose to do so. But was this a conscious, rational choice based on an assessment of available alternatives? This is only meaningful when there is a real choice from a range of appropriate alternatives. If the choice is home care, adequate support services should be there for the 'handicapped' person and the family. If the choice is institutional care, these facilities should be as good as they possibly can be[9]. Choice also implies that the family and the individual concerned are viewed as carrying major responsibility for the decision and that professionals should not impose one course of action over another even if they believe it to be more appropriate.

It was pointed out in Chapter 2 that many families in the nineteenth and early twentieth centuries kept their elderly parents in their homes, often at high social and economic costs, because the alternative, the Poor Law institution, was not acceptable. Technically there was a choice, but most families rejected it. The same was probably true of families with handicapped children in those instances when the State did not bring coercion for institutionalization. They chose this course of action, but in reality there was no choice. Are families today making more rational decisions because there are meaningful alternatives or is it possible that they are actually more disadvantaged? Since the Second World War official policy has been community care. Enabling legislation has been passed and local authorities have been encouraged to provide a full range of community support services. Families know these services exist, but coverage is limited by lack of resources. Expectations are higher now than at the turn of the century and families are conceivably more frustrated when the services are not available.

Finally, the kind of choice a caring society should provide implies a diversity of options, flexible enough to meet the families' specific needs, and available when required. In practice, choice is restricted to those services that have been developed by a local authority and in this sense, choice is limited. It is further restricted to those services that are actually available when the family makes contact with the agency. Depending on the availability of resources, families can be pressured towards institutionalization when they want to maintain the child or elderly person at home or vice versa, in so far as the process of choice may be controlled in a subtle way by the agency and not by the family. It might be argued that it is a realistic response to the periodic (or longstanding) problem of scarce resources, a practical short-term solution. While the actual service provided (whether institutional or community care) may not meet the specific needs of the family or the person with the handicap, something is being done. Even if this is granted, it is likely to create more serious problems still. Such actions can result in unnecessary institutionalizations when community services are underdeveloped, with considerable social costs to the family and the person institutionalized as well as economic costs to the State. On the other hand, if institutional care seems appropriate but facilities are limited, community care may create undue hardship for the families.

If the essence of a caring society involves the development and provision of a wide range of alternative social welfare services so that families can choose what is most appropriate for them, emphasis must be given to those policies and programmes that are basically supportive. Support in contrast to substitution will invariably involve sharing. The issue of whose responsibility it is to provide care for the mentally handicapped or the elderly can not be reduced to the simple conclusion that it is either the family's or the State's responsibility. Nor is it a matter of the family providing necessary care until this becomes impossible and then the State substituting for the family. For most of these families it is more a need for the State, through its social welfare system, to carry some of the responsibility. For those families in a position to provide the major portion of the care, sharing may entail financial assistance to offset the economic strains associated with the handicapping condition; practical help and advice related to homemaking and physical adaptations to the home; short-term relief for holidays, shopping or recreation. At another level, sharing may mean that the family will be given some assurance that if and when the burden becomes too much, when they can no longer maintain the handicapped person in the home, there will be a residential place available. Even if this were to occur, the family may continue to provide some care while their child or parent is in the institution.

These elements, the choice to maintain the handicapped member at home or to seek institutionalization, and the provision of services in such a way that families and the State share the caring function and support each other, require not only a range of services, but services that are flexible and innovative. Surveys have identified what families see to be their needs. These include relief from the pressure of providing full-time care, support in overcoming a sense of social isolation, financial assistance, transportation, housing and practical assistance. Finally an overriding concern of families is the need to feel that someone is interested, that someone cares and recognizes their contribution[10].

The problem is, of course, how to develop services that meet these criteria. It is not so much a question of volume, though this is critical, but more of building into the system flexibility, creativity, choice and responsiveness. These aspects of a caring State are not new but have been discussed for decades. Recently the Seebohm Committee[11] pointed out that while many of the problems facing the personal social services were related to inadequate levels of resources, a number of serious deficiencies were associated with the way the services were organized and delivered. Existing services were felt to be insufficiently adaptable to meeting social need (para. 16) and in some instances inappropriate services were provided (para. 77). The Committee further concluded that the services were structured in such a way that the 'nature of much social distress was ignored' (para. 142). A number of their recommendations were concerned with the importance of meeting the total needs of individuals and families, not just 'dealing with symptoms', and the necessity to deploy resources to promote wellbeing, where possible to prevent problems from occurring, and if not possible, to minimize their impact. This approach goes far beyond the residual welfare model of substitution for the family.

The critical issue becomes, then, its implementation. How likely is it that families will receive support when the pattern has been the opposite? What are the barriers?

The issue of resource constraints

The present economic situation is likely to affect public expenditure for the social services significantly. While some are arguing that current levels of provision need to be protected, others fear that there will be actual retrenchment. In responding to the crisis, the Government is proposing to reduce the level of public spending and to hold real growth to less than 3 per cent. Requests for increased funds are to be examined carefully and approved only if they are clearly 'necessary to meet inescapable commitments' and local authorities have been advised to plan only for those services that are 'strictly necessary'[12]. Furthermore, Social Service Departments have been told to 'concentrate their effort mainly on those in the most acute and immediate need: children at risk of ill-treatment, the very old and severely handicapped living alone, the mentally ill and mentally handicapped in urgent need of care and individuals and families at imminent risk of breakdown'[13]. While this policy will have serious implications for families caring for the handicapped, the current situation needs to be interpreted within a broader time frame. What has been the pattern of public expenditure on social services over the years? Are there indications that once the crisis has passed these expenditures will increase substantially?

At the turn of the century, public expenditure accounted for slightly over 14 per cent of the national income, and half of that was earmarked for defence. In the 1920s it rose to approximately 25 per cent and during the depression years, it reached 30 per cent. Expenditure on social welfare, from 1900 to 1938, grew steadily from under 3 to 11 per cent of the GNP[14].

Table 5.1 *Public expenditure and expenditure on social welfare as percentage of the gross national product, 1900—73*

Year	Social welfare expenditure	Total public expenditure
1900	2.6	14.4
1910	4.2	12.7
1920	6.8	26.2
1928	9.6	24.2
1938	11.3	30.0
1950	18.0	39.0
1961	17.6	42.8
1968	23.5	52.1
1970	23.7	50.4
1973	24.6	50.5

Note: Categories include: social security, health and personal social services, education and housing.

Sources: A. T. Peacock and J. Wiseman, *The Growth of Public Expenditures in the United Kingdom*, Oxford University Press, 1961, Tables 9 and 12; *National Income and Expenditure*, HMSO, 1963—73.

During the 1960s, public expenditure had increased to the point where it accounted for approximately 50 per cent of the national income. With the exception of periodic fluctuations in defence spending (e.g. the Suez crisis), this trend in public expenditure can be directly attributed to the increased role of government in the provision of social services, currently accounting for one-half of all public expenditure and one-fourth of the gross national product (GNP).

While this growth pattern in social welfare expenditure existed in the prewar period, over the first forty years of this century, one-half of the expenditure went to various income transfer programmes and one-fourth to education. The remaining 25 per cent was distributed among the health, housing and personal social service sectors. Since the war this distribution has shifted only marginally[15].

Table 5.2   Per capita *expenditure on social welfare, United Kingdom (£s)*

	1953	*1958*	*1963*	*1968*	*1972*
NHS	19.46	21.82	26.95	35.07	40.55
Social security	33.33	40.32	51.76	69.39	78.50
Education	17.29	23.54	33.37	45.33	53.78
Housing	21.25	12.57	15.42	23.46	22.23
Personal social services	1.30	1.50	2.13	3.28	5.89
School meals, milk and welfare foods	2.92	2.37	2.71	3.19	2.51
Total social welfare	95.55	102.12	132.34	179.72	203.46
Total public expenditure	250.55	249.05	303.74	397.58	416.23

Notes: *Per capita* expenditures are expressed in constant prices, 1970 base.
While *per capita* expenditure more appropriately would use specific population rather than total population, e.g. *per capita* expenditures for education would be related to the population using education services, the use of total population can be justified since the purpose is to show general trends.

Source: Adapted from R. Klein *et al., Social Policy and Public Expenditure, 1974,* London, Centre for Studies in Social Policy, 1974, Table 3.

For example, social security expenditure has dropped to slightly under 40 per cent of all social welfare expenditure and spending on education has remained at the 25 per cent level. Expenditure on the National Health Service from 1953 to 1972 changed little in its share of the total resources (20 per cent). Spending on the personal social services showed significant increases: in 1953 its share was slightly over 1 per cent, by 1972, 3 per cent, but this has to be tempered by the fact that earlier expenditure was minimal. Housing was the one sector that showed a relative decrease in expenditure (22 per cent in 1953 and 11 per cent in 1972).

Looking at real growth in each sector, it becomes apparent that over the twenty years the priorities have not changed (with the notable exception of housing, showing an increase of 5 per cent, and the personal social services: the increase here was significant, 353 per cent, but the starting point was so low in 1953). The increase in expenditure on education was 211 per cent; on social security 135 per cent, and on health, 108 per cent.

Over the past twenty years, *per capita* national income has increased by 52 per cent in real terms, *per capita* public expenditure by 66 per cent and *per capita* expenditure on social welfare by 113 per cent. As discussed in Chapters 3 and 4, these increases can be translated into considerable expansion in services for the elderly and the mentally handicapped. Based on the criterion of rates of growth in social welfare expenditure, it can be argued that the State has demonstrated a commitment to meeting social need, and has given high priority to this sector of public expenditure.

Although there have been considerable increases in public expenditure on social services, serious shortages still exist. In fact, in some services the increases have barely kept abreast of general population growth, and in others the increases in utilization have outstripped manpower growth, resulting in a less effective service. For example, in terms of services for the elderly there is still a shortage of over 25,000 residential care places (assuming the DHSS target of twenty-five places per 1,000 elderly). Assuming a goal of twelve home helps per 1,000 elderly, there is an estimated shortfall of 44,000 home helps, more than double the current number, and even then this increase would only meet minimal needs. Meals services need to be doubled to cover known need and even this coverage would not guarantee that the nutritional needs of the elderly would be met[16].

The State has also identified a number of serious shortages in services for the mentally handicapped. In 1969 over 33,000 additional residential care places were estimated to be needed, 3,000 for children and the remainder for adults. It was further believed that day-care places for children under the age of six needed to be increased by 600 per cent and places in adult training centres by 50,000[17]. These are just a few of the services needed by two 'at risk' groups and shortages of this scale can be found in almost all the social services.

A number of dimensions of this issue are important to this study. In spite of the considerable growth in social welfare expenditure over the past twenty years there are still critical shortages, and these shortages are continuing to be felt most heavily by the families who are carrying the major responsibility for their handicapped parents and children. While these families are in a better position than their counterparts of the 1940s and 1950s in so far as many of the community services either did not exist or were in their infancy, compared to other 'at risk' groups, they are seen to be 'less needy'.

If these families received lower priority in the past, their status in all probability will deteriorate over the next few years given the Government's decision to reduce public spending and its charge to local authorities to concentrate their effort on those in the most acute and immediate need. In deciding on this policy of retrenchment the State had few feasible options. Given scarce resources, administrators are confronted with a dilemma. Within limits services could be rationed by stretching the existing supply. Intake to the agencies is kept open but each recipient is provided with fewer services. The danger inherent in this strategy is that such an allocation policy is likely to result in the recipient receiving a level of service that is judged to be below the minimal required. Eventually, the effectiveness of these watered-down services would be affected and few would benefit.

Another alternative is to ration the limited supply by providing them to a smaller number of recipients. A hierarchy of relative need could be developed that would establish priorities among groups and an effective level of service could be provided to those considered in the greatest need. As with most dilemmas, each option has its cost.

Central Government has recommended to local authorities that they take the latter course, that they establish priorities and concentrate their efforts on those in the most 'acute and immediate need'. Although families caring for the handicapped are under severe strain and are in need of support, it can be argued that they have managed in the past and will probably continue to manage until the economic situation improves.

There are a number of assumptions behind this decision. First it is not considered feasible either politically or administratively to meet new need by redistributing existing resources. A significant proportion of these resources are existing facilities, hospitals, schools and homes for the elderly. They cannot be relocated and any attempt to change their function will prove difficult. Manpower, while more flexible and mobile in theory, is almost as intractable. In turn, this means that any new commitment is dependent on achieving a high rate of economic growth. As additional resources become available, they can be diverted to new programmes[18]. While the assumption that economic growth is a prerequisite for expansion in the social services has been contested[19], the association has had an historical link. The large increase in social welfare expenditure during the mid-1960s was preceded by a period of considerable growth in the national income[20] and similarly, the present period has following on a period of relatively low economic growth.

This situation has an interesting parallel in recent history. In his classic study of social policy during the war years Titmuss graphically showed that while the nation as a whole was expected to share the costs of the war effort, some groups were required to pay a higher price. Military personnel and production workers were given the highest priority for scarce health and welfare services, a practice that was probably acceptable to most of the population. These people were more essential to the country's survival.

The successful mobilization of the emergency medical service did, however, result in serious delays for admission to hospitals, inappropriate discharges, and lower standards of care for the civilian population. Inadequate services for the physically ill were paralleled in hospitals for the mentally ill and mentally handicapped. More than 25,000 beds in these institutions were taken over by the emergency medical service, causing severe overcrowding problems[21]. It has been estimated that a significant number of mentally handicapped persons needing hospital care were not admitted and many who were patients at that time were discharged. Titmuss suggested that the price paid for this decision was 'much suffering to themselves (the handicapped), to their families and to the community'. Instead of an equitable sharing of the cost of the crisis:

It is clear that children, far from occupying a privileged position in the war-time hospitals, had to make their contribution to the social cost of the emergency medical service. At the other end of the age scale, elderly and old people were compelled to make an even larger contribution to the success of the service.... The sacrifices imposed ... in the interests of Britain's war effort took two forms: more of them were excluded from hospital care, and a proportion of those admitted had to accept inferior standards[22].

While the current crisis (1975) is economic rather than military, in both cases it is a question of resource allocation and its impact on the social services is likely to be the same. The policy options were limited then as they are now, and priorities had to be established. Some groups received services, others received inadequate services, and many received little if anything. The mentally handicapped and the elderly were required to pay a disproportionate cost during the 1940s. Who will be required to make the sacrifice in the 1970s? Will the sharing be more equitable?

Following the Government's current policy of general retrenchment, families caring for the handicapped in their homes and receiving little support during the expansionary periods of the 1960s, are likely to receive less in the near future. While the nation was asked to sacrifice, to pay the price for survival during the war years, they were given some assurances that once the crisis was over adequate resources would become available to achieve social objectives. Their sacrifice was explicitly recognized. Do families caring for their handicapped children and elderly parents need a similar commitment that recognizes their effort now? What guarantee do they have that the State will meet their needs once the economic situation is reversed? And finally, is the only barrier a lack of resources or are there other issues of equal importance?

It is somewhat simplistic to assume that once the economic crisis is reversed and the country enters another expansionary period social services will be plentiful enough to filter down to families caring for the handicapped. Such a rationale suggests that the needs of these families can only be met after the State has provided services to those in more acute situations — the elderly living alone, children in danger of being abused, the mentally handicapped without families. Such a position is based on a number of questionable premises and grounded firmly in analyses of supply and demand. Trends in utilization can provide some idea of demand patterns and when linked to an analysis of the characteristics of the recipients and demographic projections, provide a reasonable estimate of what demand might be in the future. When related to estimates of need, the total data set can be translated into specific service requirements necessary to eliminate existing shortages.

However, reliance on these projections can be dangerous. On the one hand, supply and demand relationships are based on historical trends — a reflection of what occurred in the past. Need, on the other hand, is much more complex and difficult to measure. While indicators may be derived from expert opinion, research and surveys, they are, at best, estimates of what need is thought to be at the moment, and what it might be if attitudes, expectations and behaviour do not change. Examples of these estimates are the number of places in homes for the elderly or hostels for the mentally handicapped, the number of meals on wheels, home helps, social workers, and health visitors.

And yet these projections, based on a relationship between supply and demand that is assumed to be linear, and furthermore, a belief that need will remain at some constant level, are quite limited[23]. For example, it was pointed out in Chapter 3 that over a ten-year period each percentage increase in home helps, health visitors and home nurses, brought with it a 2 per cent increase in the number of people receiving these services. Were the increases mainly a reflection of the large backlog of people waiting for services or was the increase in service actually triggering new demand? While there have been significant increases in the number of residential care places for the elderly since 1952 (160 per cent) these institutions are always working at close to full capacity[24]. As more places became available, they were filled. How many places would be sufficient to meet need? Were these new residents already known to the local authorities and did they merely move from waiting-lists, or is it possible that increases in resources were, in fact, creating new demand? While waiting-list statistics must be viewed with caution there is some indication that the latter is occurring. The number of elderly people on waiting-lists for residential care appears to have remained constant. As people leave the waiting-list, they are replaced[25].

The factors associated with this are complex and probably vary between local authorities. One reason may be that increases in services are raising expectations and this in turn is being translated into demand. If it is known that there are limited resources and that waiting-lists are lengthy, it is conceivable that many will not see the value of applying for help. If, on the other hand, people find that additional services are available, they may be more willing to apply. Another facet of this relationship between supply and expectation is possibly linked to changes in perception. A family may have been willing to carry on without support from the social welfare system and then demand services when they find that a neighbour or friend in a similar situation has received something[26]. Once a benefit or service becomes available, or if standards in existing services are improved sufficiently so that they are thought to be more acceptable, expectations are likely to be raised. A final factor may be linked to the definition of need used. For example, many of the proposed targets for services for the elderly are derived from Harris's survey of the elderly and the handicapped. According to her study, 27 per cent of the elderly were impaired and slightly less than 2 per cent severely handicapped. Townsend however reported higher levels of incapacity (45 per cent) and severe incapacity (6 per cent). As discussed in Chapter 3, one explanation of this variation could be related to definitions used and how incapacity or handicap was measured. The former reported on 'tested ability', the latter on 'perceived ability'. While Harris's data are conceivably more reliable and measure clinical need, Townsend's findings, based on what people think they are capable of doing, suggest that additional demand for services will continue even if the proposed levels of provision were to be achieved.

While these are only a few of the factors, they suggest that current estimates of need must be treated with caution[27]. There is every likelihood that once a level of provision has been achieved it will in the process have generated new demand and the targets will require readjusting. The critical issue is not that the adjustment will have to be made, but rather that in establishing new priorities, families will find themselves in no better position than they were before.

Organizational barriers to the provision of services

There are other limitations to an approach based on supply, demand and needs analysis. While guidelines for service provision are rarely proposed as a set plan of action, once developed and promulgated they have a tendency to become the detailed operational blueprint. Having been decided on, the various programmes often became ends in themselves, rather than the instruments to achieve some objective. They generate their own dynamism and can reduce efforts to initiate change through more flexible experimentation in as much as the emphasis tends to shift to organizational survival. In turn, administrators who are responsible for the management of programmes structure their agencies in such a way that the purpose of the organization may become the sum total of their service components. Social welfare staff in local authorities will tend to view a potential client in terms of what services they are in a position to offer. The elderly for example are defined as 'needing' home help services, meals, places in residential accommodations or some form of medical care. The mentally handicapped 'require' residential care, special education, places in training centres, assessment and rehabilitation services. Whatever the system, this labelling begins at intake, and continues throughout contact with the agency. Needs are translated invariably into what a particular agency has to offer. While this is an overstatement, as a pattern it is commonly found in most bureaucracies. Flexibility may exist but it is usually limited to a successful manipulation of the existing service package. Titmuss observed:

Boards of Governors and Management Committees devote more of their time to conditions of work, questions of rewards, difficulties of status and dissatisfaction among the staff than they do to meet the needs of the patients. Of course, all of these questions are vital to the efficient and harmonious running of a hospital; there must be a system of settling these often difficult issues. . . . One of the new problems is the danger that the hospital may tend increasingly to be run in the interests of those working in and for the hospital rather than in the interests of the patients. The fundamental purpose of the hospital must not be dimmed by excessive preoccupation with the means[28].

This conclusion is not unique to the hospital sector and can be found in most agencies. A recent comment in *New Society* raised the same warning:

When the NUT complains about the education services, and the BMA criticizes the level of expenditure on health care, are they really concerned with the pupil and patient? Or is it the income and working conditions of their members they are worried about? . . . Social Services Committees, when called to make cuts, don't sack social workers or reduce their salaries: they tend to make reductions in direct services like aids and adaptations for handicapped children, financial support to various voluntary organizations, or home helps[29].

For any number of reasons, whether organizational requirements or professional satisfaction, services that were introduced initially as possible mechanisms to assist people with need, quickly become *the* way to do things. Services that were seen as potentially of benefit became solutions whose benefit is rarely questioned. Innovation is replaced with caution, and flexibility with formal structures.

The Seebohm Committee in their landmark Report argued that the existing social welfare system was so structured that many social problems could not be dealt with effectively. The system itself was fragmented and most of the service agencies were hampered by severe shortages in resources. Compounding this were the inadequacies in the range and quality of services that were available. Furthermore, there was little evidence of coordination between agencies, difficult access to services and a rigid approach to problem solving[30]. They then recommended the development of a 'new local authority department providing a community based and family oriented service which would be available to all'[31].

It was felt that by consolidating the resources from a number of previously independent departments, this new personal social service department would be in a position to attract more resources, including highly qualified manpower; would be more flexible, accessible and comprehensive than the existing system; and finally would be able to meet the needs of people more efficiently and more effectively.

The ideas generated in the Report were precisely those that could benefit those families who are caring for the handicapped: a family oriented service, one that would give high priority to those living in the community, a system that was to be flexible, accessible, comprehensive and available to all sections of the population[32]. In 1970, the then Secretary of State for Social Services during the Commons debate on the reorganization of the personal social services stated that:

The primary objective of the personal social services we can best describe as strengthening the capacity of the family to care for its members and to supply, as it were, the family's place where necessary: that is to provide as far as may be social support, or if necessary a home for people who cannot

*look after themselves or be adequately looked after in their family. This is
not the only objective of the personal social services . . . but it has been
the idea of forming a 'family' service that has inspired the call for a review
of the organization of the services in which the Bill is concerned [emphasis
added]* [33].

This approach, reiterating the Ingleby Report mentioned earlier,
implicitly assumes that the family and the State should share the caring
function. Whereas in earlier periods the State may have viewed its proper
function as one of intervention only when the family was incapable or
unwilling to provide care (a residual approach) the role of the State was
clearly expanded to offer supportive services to families while they were
providing care. At least at the conceptual level, priorities had been re-
arranged. The question that now needs to be raised is whether the philosophical framework and the enabling legislation have brought about
changes in actual practice.

The reorganization has been successful in meeting some of the objectives proposed by the Seebohm Committee. The new departments have
been able to attract more resources, increases that probably would not
have been significant without reorganization. Since 1970 the rate of
growth in expenditure on the personal social services has been significantly
higher than those in other social welfare sectors. Increases in resources and
a new organizational structure with the potential to translate these
increases into effective services are two key dimensions, but only two. A
third component is the attitude and behaviour of those persons in direct
contact with the recipient, the staff responsible for actually providing the
services. The three resources, structure and practice, cannot be separated
and each will have an influence on the overall effect of improving the
status of families with handicapped members.

Manpower: the critical role of the social worker

Throughout the Seebohm Report and in subsequent Government docu-
ments, the social worker has been identified as the key service provider,
the person best placed to ensure a family focus, to carry out the assessment of need, to mobilize necessary resources, and to carry the overall
responsibility for appropriate coordination of effort both within the
department and between agencies[34]. Before reorganization, social
workers in the various local authority agencies were seen as functioning at
a distinct disadvantage in so far as they had little actual control over the
total range of needed social services, or resources, or they lacked sufficient
knowledge and skills[35]. Given the thrust of reorganization, these
limitations should have been eliminated at least in part.

Despite the lack of systematic and national information related to this
issue of practice, available data suggest that the hoped for changes have
not occurred on a large scale[36]. Families caring for the elderly and the
mentally handicapped receive less priority relative to other 'at risk' groups.

This conclusion is quite different from one arguing that the elderly and mentally handicapped do not receive an equitable share of the personal social services. For example, in 1971–72, personal social service expenditure on the elderly accounted for 44 per cent of all local authority spending in this sector, for the physically handicapped almost 8 per cent, and for the mentally ill and mentally handicapped slightly over 9 per cent. Two-thirds of the expenditure for the elderly and a large percentage of that for the mentally handicapped went to residential care services. Expenditure on community social services is recognized to be low compared to the institutional services, even though the volume of services such as home help and meals on wheels has increased. Given the estimated shortages and the existing waiting-lists, the elderly and the mentally handicapped are likely to be regarded as 'priority areas' only after the family is unable or unwilling to continue providing support. Relatively little is made available to families until they reach the breaking point, and often the only course open is placement in an institution. The emphasis on 'strengthening the capacity of the family to care for its members' by the Seebohm Committee and the Secretary of State has not been achieved. Current practice still reflects an emphasis on providing services that substitute for the family (whether institutional or community services), or services geared to intervening in crisis situations.

The reasons for this are complex. The one raised most often by social workers is the lack of resources. Reorganization brought high visibility and raised public expectations. This, together with new legislation such as the Children's and Young Persons Act, 1969, and the Chronically Sick and Disabled Persons Act, has resulted in considerable increases in demand without accompanying increases in resources, bringing about a serious imbalance. Social workers argue that they are faced with unmanageable caseloads and less than adequate support services necessary to achieve the desired objectives underlying the formation of the new departments. (The issue of caseloads is discussed later in the chapter.) Crisis situations take up most of their time and families who seem to be managing, albeit under considerable strain, are not crisis situations in the ordinary sense for they have learned to adjust and to develop coping mechanisms. Social workers further point to tremendous pressures they are experiencing in child care cases now that local authorities have the statutory responsibility to protect the wellbeing of children in danger of physical abuse. Many feel that this requires a considerable investment of time and resources, involving close supervision, frequent home visiting and continuous communication with other agencies. Social workers are afraid that if resources were diverted from child care to other groups, it is possible that a number of children would be battered or killed. If resources are not made available to families caring for handicapped children or elderly parents, the probability is that the families will still be able to manage, at least for a time. Their conclusion is that unless more resources are found, practitioners will have to emphasize crisis or emergency situations and families with management problems will have to wait.

The above is a fairly accurate reflection of how those involved in the delivery of the personal social services, especially the social workers, view the problem and there is a great deal of truth to the argument that resources are inadequate. It is much too easy and simplistic a solution to suggest that social workers divert some of their efforts to other groups. No one can reasonably expect them to turn away or defer crisis situations. They are real and they exist. However, there is probably more than resources involved, and it could be hypothesized that even with more resources available to local authorities families might still not receive the services they need. The rhetoric of services to strengthen families is one thing, its implementation another. It involves a rearrangement of patterns of care, a rethinking of the role of the practitioner and the skills necessary to achieve it. Social workers, physicians and other professionals in the social services, trained in the clinical model, are conditioned to recognize pathology. While some attention in professional education may be given to preventive care and normal growth and development, the overriding emphasis is on the successful treatment and reversal of problems. Many of the families who care for the handicapped are not faced with acute crises, rather they are normal families who are under pressure from long-term, chronic management problems. They require support and need to feel that someone is interested in them. They want someone to take the time to listen and to provide them with useful information. Finally, they need relief and practical help. Because their needs are 'ordinary or even mundane', social workers, physicians, nurses and other professionals often do not see these families as 'interesting cases' from which they can receive professional satisfaction.

In dealing with child care cases or homeless families, the social worker possibly is in a position to reverse the pathology. The child is protected either through intensive work with the parents, or if necessary by removing the child from the family. Successful intervention with families providing care for the handicapped is not of the same dramatic order and different criteria have to be used.

Another facet is that many social workers lack substantive knowledge about the ageing process and mental handicap and their impact on families[37]. Whether this has been influenced by the recent emphasis on generic social work practice or integrated case loads, deficiencies in the training of staff, or the high annual turnover of field practitioners, the result is that many social workers appear to be uneasy in dealing with the handicapped and their families. There is probably some degree of carry-over from the pre-Seebohm era when specialization was the norm and social workers were reluctant to choose a career working with the elderly or with the mentally handicapped. Whatever the reasons, the way in which manpower is recruited and deployed will in part determine whether or not families providing care for the dependent will receive required services.

It has been suggested that the social services are now faced with a more knowledgeable public who have much higher expectations than previously, as well as with the explicit policy of community care that has resulted in large-scale discharges from various institutions. The need is, and will continue to be, a disproportionate expansion (compared to institutional resources) in the community social services, e.g. health and rehabilitation, home care, day care, community centres, advice and counselling. While such an emphasis on community care is dependent on the willingness to channel resources to various programmes, its overall impact will be affected by the local authority's ability to recruit and deploy the manpower required to provide these services. What kind of manpower is involved and where will it come from?

In 1973 local authority personal social service departments in England employed almost 150,000 persons at a cost of £265 million. For every 100 social workers there were 221 home helps and organizers, 185 manual and domestic workers, 166 residential care staff for the elderly and 69 residential care staff for children, 59 staff working in day nurseries and day centres and 65 administrative and clerical staff[38]. If there is to be expansion over the next five to ten years where will it be? In discussing this issue with administrators and planners in local authorities and central Government as well as with social service academicians, it seems that priority should be given to two groups — field social workers and residential care staff. The rationale for this is understandable. Social workers, representing slightly over 11 per cent of all social service staff, are the key personnel in the existing system. They are responsible for assessing the needs of consumers, for locating appropriate resources and effecting referrals to those services, for coordinating and monitoring intra- and inter-departmental service delivery. Furthermore, when required, they provide advice and counselling. And yet, in 1973–74 less than four of every ten field social workers were 'qualified' in the sense of having completed some form of recognized training and education. Residential care staff, for their part, are required to provide a complex range of supportive and thera-peutic services to children, the physically and mentally handicapped, and the elderly. Yet in 1973–74, only 4 per cent of residential staff had professional training.

Given these shortages, emphasis on professional training and upgrading of skills is defensible. However, if the greater share of the anticipated resources were to be allocated to these two groups, the outcome could seriously limit the overall effectiveness of the local authority's efforts. This proposed policy appears to be based on a number of untested assumptions. The first and most basic is that professionally trained staff are more effective than those who are not trained. Such a generalization is indefen-sible, yet it is widely held. While professionals are likely to be the appro-priate staff to carry out some functions, they are not the best equipped staff to carry out others. For example, those arguing for more trained social workers on the basis of unmanageable caseloads, seem to ignore the fact that up to one-third of the social worker's time is spent on clerical tasks[39]. Many of the social services can be provided by less qualified personnel. However, to move beyond the rhetoric would require that the functions of the department would have to be identified and broken down into concrete tasks. If this were to happen then decisions could be made as to which tasks are appropriate to specific levels of training.

A second assumption is that trained staff are not only more effective problem solvers whose knowledge and skills should be centred on an appropriate use of their time, but that the professionally qualified in turn can raise the level of practice among the less qualified. To achieve this, tasks would have to be delegated and the professionally trained would have to assume a supervisory responsibility. However, many professionals for a number of reasons find this responsibility an uncomfortable one and feel ill-equipped to carry it out. The time involved is significant and while delegation may free the professional from certain types of work, they argue that the time gained is then absorbed in supervision and they are not free to work more intensely with families or individuals.

Accompanying this problem of delegation and supervision is the equally troublesome issue of status. If one category of staff is given higher status, those with lower status in the same organization may become resentful or, even more damaging, they may attempt to emulate those with the higher status. This is already occurring in some local authorities. Many home helps, dissatisfied with their perceived lower status, are suggesting that they should de-emphasize and reduce the 'domestic help' aspects of the job and provide more counselling. While 'counselling' is probably beneficial the elderly and others with handicaps have more need for help with cleaning, shopping, meals and other aspects of homemaking. It is these services that often make the difference in terms of living in the community or having to go into an institution.

For these reasons policies emphasizing the upgrading of social work and residential care staff can be counterproductive. There are shortages of qualified staff in these key positions and few will argue against improving this situation. The danger is that such an approach will result in a neglect of other equally critical shortages, such as the home helps and the social work assistants. Even if the number of trained social workers were to be increased significantly over the next ten years, their effectiveness would be seriously hampered if their efforts were not complemented by adequate numbers of non-social work staff.

One final aspect of the manpower issue should be touched on, however briefly. While it is recognized that the State may have an overall responsibility to meet the needs of its citizens, a responsibility that has come to include both supportive as well as substitution functions, this does not mean that these functions are to be carried out only through the existing network of governmental agencies. Furthermore, State responsibility does not necessarily imply that all those involved in the provision of caring services must be employed by the State. Just as some tasks can be undertaken by non-professional staff, so also certain tasks can be carried out by volunteers. By actively recruiting and channelling the efforts of volunteers, local authority departments can actually initiate a process with far-reaching impact. Given the estimated shortages of all levels of social service staff, the careful integration of volunteers can relieve some of the existing pressure and demand. Programmes such as the pilot 'good neighbour' schemes and the use of volunteers in day centres for the handicapped have demonstrated their value. Furthermore, by encouraging people to volunteer, local authorities could be instrumental in stimulating a sense of community among people resulting in a 'network of reciprocal social relationships which among other things ensure mutual aid and gives those who experience it a sense of well-being'[40].

The Seebohm Committee in their Report argued that the proposed local authority personal social service departments should become the focal point for those wishing to volunteer their services, yet, six years after the Report and four years after the creation of the new departments, this has not been achieved[41]. To be fair, local authorities have had significant pressures on them — the reorganization itself required new structures to be developed and staff to be integrated into these structures; legislation continually placed increased responsibilities on the local authorities; and finally the demand for services that followed. Still, given the present climate and the prospect of little or no growth these departments might seriously extend their effort toward the recruitment of volunteers. Potentially, it could prove of great benefit to families caring for the elderly or the mentally handicapped.

Summary

This chapter began by raising the question of the State's responsibility to meet social need in general, and specifically its relationship to families with handicapped members. It was suggested that if patterns of expenditure were used as an indicator of commitment, the State has demonstrated its social concern despite the fact that serious shortages still exist. However, reliance on this form of analysis can be misleading and counterproductive. It assumes that solutions are known and ultimately social need will be met if an adequate amount of resources become available. Furthermore, it is based on an idea that need is known and will remain constant. Yet there is every likelihood that as the State provides more services it will be called on to make greater and greater provision. Increases in services may heighten expectation and trigger new demand, and need itself must be viewed as relative and fluid. Furthermore 'caring' does not mean just more of the same types of services.

In spite of significant expansion in the social services, families providing care for handicapped parents or mentally handicapped children are still receiving fewer services relative to other groups. While the State has explicitly stated that its primary function is to strengthen the capacity of families and, when that is not possible, to substitute for the family, this secondary role is still emphasized. Some of the factors associated with this were seen as a lack of resources, the way services are structured, and finally, the attitudes of the people responsible for providing the services. It was argued that the three were interdependent and improvement would require more than additional resources. A number of criteria were proposed if services were to in fact 'strengthen the capacity of families', including choice from a number of options, flexibility of approach, and an operational commitment to supportive services that share the caring responsibility instead of substituting for the family.

The next chapter discusses these concepts in a broader context of future policy choices, including income maintenance and housing policies, and the overriding issue of family policy.

References

1. Beveridge is recognized as one of the most articulate defenders of the principle of universal services. He argued the need for a national insurance plan '. . . to insure at all times to all men a subsistence income for themselves and their families as of right; that is to say, without any form of means test or inquiry about other means they had', *Hansard* (Lords), 1953, **182**, cols 675–6. Proponents of the selective approach do not explicitly criticize the principle of State responsibility. They do argue that, given scarce resources, only those needing assistance should be helped, see, for example, I. MacLeod and J. E. Powell, *The Social Services — Needs and Means*, Conservative Political Centre, 1958; also see M. Reddin, 'Universality versus selectivity', in *The Future of the Social Services*, eds, W. Robson and B. Crick, Penguin, 1970, for a discussion of the implications of services based on these approaches.

2. Beveridge was primarily concerned with establishing an income floor below which no one would fall. He also argued that individuals should be encouraged to supplement this through various private insurance schemes. Titmuss, on the other hand, proposed that social policy and the social services should go beyond minimum guarantees and government should actively seek to reduce social inequalities and to improve the quality of life in a society. See *Essays on the Welfare State*, Allen and Unwin, 1958.

3. One expression of this argument begins with the assumption that social services cannot be provided through market mechanisms. The aims of social services do not lend themselves to supply, demand and profit factors. The counter position suggests that over time there should be conscious government action to reduce the amount of public social services in favour of private sector provision. See, for example, G. Howe, 'Reform of the social services', in *Principles and Practice*, Bow Group Publication, 1961.

4. T. H. Marshall, *Social Policy*, Hutchinson University Library, 1965, p. 97.

5. For example, the State has the legal power under Section 47 of the National Assistance Act, 1948, to 'remove to suitable premises persons in need of care and attention', and under Sections 1 and 2 of the Children's Act, 1948, to empower local authorities to 'receive into care a child under 17 if he is without parents or if his parents, temporarily or permanently, are for some reason unable to provide for his proper accommodation, maintenance and upbringing, and if reception into care would be in the interest of the child's welfare'. This principle was reaffirmed by the Children and Young Persons Act, 1969, and the Mental Health Act, 1959.

6. R. Titmuss, *Social Policy*, Allen and Unwin, 1963, p. 133.

7. *Report of the Committee on Children and Young Persons*, Cmnd 1191, HMSO, 1960, p. 8.

8. See for example: R. Klein and P. Hall, *Caring for Quality in the Caring Services*, London, Centre for Studies in Social Policy, Bedford Square Press, 1974; R. Morris, *Toward a Caring Society*, Columbia University School of Social Work, 1974.

9. There are any number of reports that identify the range of services required by populations at risk. These would include E. Young-husband, *et al.*, *Living with Handicap*, London, National Children's Bureau, 1971; DHSS, *Better Services for the Mentally Handicapped*, Cmnd 4683, HMSO, 1971; various manifestos published by Age Concern; *The Report of the Committee on Local Authority and Allied Personal Social Services*, Cmnd 3703, HMSO, 1968.

10. *Living with Handicap* op. cit. (ref. 9), includes letters from parents with handicapped children. Their comments and those of families cited in the studies of S. Hewitt and M. Bayley (see Ch. 4, refs 19 and 26) provide valuable insight for anyone concerned with the problems of service provision.

11. *Report of the Committee on Local Authority and Allied Personal Services*, Cmnd 3703, HMSO, 1968.

12. Joint Circular, *Rate Fund Expenditure and the Rate Call in 1975–1976*, 23 December 1974.

13. Ibid.

14. A. T. Peacock and J. Wiseman, *The Growth of Public Expenditure in the United Kingdom*, Oxford University Press, 1961, Tables 9 and 12.

15. For an interesting analysis of this growth see: J. F. Sleeman, *The Welfare State: Its Aims, Benefits and Costs*, Allen and Unwin, 1973.

16. DHSS, Circular 35/72. *Local Authority Social Services Ten Year Development Plans 1973–1983*, 31 August 1972.

17. DHSS, *Better Services for the Mentally Handicapped*, Cmnd 4683, HMSO, 1971, p. 42.

18. See D. Donnison, 'Social work and social change', *British Journal of Psychiatric Social Work*, **8**, no. 4, 1966, pp. 3—9; L. Keyserling, 'The problem of problems: economic growth', in *Social Policies for America in the Seventies*, ed. R. Theobald, New York, Anchor Books, 1969, pp. 1—24.

19. For example see R. Titmuss, 'Social policy and economic progress', *Commitment to Welfare*, Allen and Unwin, 1968, pp. 153—65; J. K. Galbraith, *The Affluent Society*, Boston, Houghton Mifflin, 1958.

20. A. T. Peacock and J. Wiseman, op. cit. (ref. 14), Tables 9 and 12.

21. R. Titmuss, *Problems of Social Policy*, HMSO and Longmans, 1950, pp. 490, 497.

22. Ibid., pp. 498, 499—500.

23. J. Bradshaw offers an interesting discussion of the concept of need in 'The concept of social need', *New Society*, 30 March 1972, pp. 640—3.

24. Occupancy rates have consistently been at the 95 to 98 per cent level nationally. This level of 'full occupancy' might be counterproductive to the stated policy of maintaining some places for short-term stays whose purpose is to provide relief for families.

25. Based on recent communication with a number of local authorities.

26. This hypothesis was suggested by an executive of a national voluntary organization concerned with the handicapped. Following the creation of the Family Fund, a programme offering support to families with congenitally handicapped children, this agency received a large number of calls from families demanding help. They argued that families with children like their own had been given assistance while their applications had been rejected. Similarly, many families who had been found ineligible for the constant attendance allowance, pointed out that other families in similar circumstances were receiving it.

27. The Department of Health and Social Security underlines this point in Circular 35/72 (see ref. 16): 'The plans now requested are not to be regarded as setting a final and inflexible forward plan for the decade. They will be subject to later review and revision and their precision and value will constantly be improved as better methods of forecasting needs and the development of services become available, as knowledge about the effectiveness of services increases and as changes and developments take place in the policy and methods they employ' (para. 6).

28. R. Titmuss, *Essays on the Welfare State*, Allen and Unwin, 1963, pp. 122—3.

29. 'Whose interests?', *New Society*, **32**, no. 659, 22 May 1975, p. 460.

30. *Report of the Committee on Local Authority and Allied Personal Social Services*, op. cit. (ref. 9), Ch. 5.

31. Ibid., para. 2.

32. In fact a number of chapters in the Report were devoted to the particular needs of the handicapped and their families. The theme throughout was that a unified social service department would be capable of assuming the overall, long-term responsibility for the social care of the handicapped individual and his family, a responsibility that would include the provision of advice, support and treatment as well as the coordination of effort between agencies.

33. *Hansard* (Commons), 26 February 1970, col. 1407.

34. For example, *Better Services for the Mentally Handicapped*, op. cit. (ref. 9), para. 141.

35. These were the conclusions reached by: J. Moncrieff (ref. 19, Ch. 4); M. Bayley (ref. 19, Ch. 4); S. Hewitt (ref. 26, Ch. 4); E. Goldberg, *et al.*, *Helping the Aged*, Allen and Unwin, 1971.

36. The comments that follow are based on a series of interviews carried out in a number of local authorities in 1974. Discussions were held with almost 100 local authority staff, including management, advisers, field social workers, residential and domiciliary care staff, teachers in special schools and training centres. Furthermore, contact was made with a number of parent groups. Since the observations were not based on a representative sample, the findings cannot be treated as a reflection of general practice. However, they undoubtedly represent a significant slice of reality.

37. Central Council for the Education and Training of Social Workers, *People with Handicaps Need Better Trained Workers*, CCETSW, Paper 5, August 1974, para. 38.

38. The Chartered Institute of Public Finance and Accountancy, *Social Services Statistics Estimates, 1974/75*, London, October 1975.

39. V. Carver and J. L. Edwards, *Social Workers and Their Workloads*, London, National Institute for Social Work Training, 1972.

40. Report of the Committee on Local Authority and Allied Personal Social Services, op. cit. (ref. 9), paras 476 and 498.

41. See for example, C. Ball, 'A voluntary spectrum', *New Society*, **32**, no. 663, 19 June 1975, pp. 714–15.

6 The family, the State and social policy

This enquiry began with the proposition that the entire structure of the Welfare State depends on a set of implicit and explicit assumptions concerning the responsibility which families carry, or are expected to carry, for the care of the socially dependent, and the conditions under which this responsibility will be shared with or taken over by society. Furthermore, it was pointed out that even though the principle of societal responsibility has been clearly articulated and a broad consensus exists that such a function is appropriate, there is still a great deal of ambiguity as to what this actually entails. The translation of the principle of societal responsibility into a coherent system of social policies has proved and is proving to be elusive. It was suggested also that although Government may shape much of its policy, legislation and programmatic development on an assumed set of relationships between the family and the State, two fundamental social institutions, these assumptions have not been analysed in a systematic fashion.

One point of view that appears to be gaining considerable momentum is that as the State assumes more responsibility for assuring that basic social and economic needs are met, the traditional responsibility of the family to provide for the needs of its members is diminished and the family as a social institution becomes less important. Children are becoming less inclined to support their elderly parents, and parents their severely disabled children. Why should they provide care, often involving personal social and economic costs, when another social institution is willing to? This line of reasoning poses the moral dimension of the argument and pre-supposes some idea of what a family should be doing. This concern is also raised in economic terms. If this has begun to occur, or if there is reason to believe that it might, what scale of additional societal or governmental resources might be required to substitute for the family? This position has been stated in exaggerated terms but variations .of it are found increasingly. It is an exaggeration only in so far as the argument is posed in extremes: the responsibility to provide social care is either the State's or the family's. The issue itself is real and has serious implications for evolving social policy.

In attempting to deal with this issue a number of questions were raised. Is there any evidence to support this view that families are increasingly transferring the caring function to the State? How does the State in practice relate to the family? Are there reasonable boundaries to the sharing of responsibility between the two? Is it possible that as more social welfare services become available, the family on the one hand is inadvertently discouraged from, or on the other hand supported and encouraged to continue, participation in the caring function? Finally, are social policies based on a realistic understanding of the family or are they built on a concept that is outmoded, or one that never existed?

Rather than attempting to deal explicitly with the socially dependent, a term that almost defies meaningful definition, the focus of the study was narrowed to families with handicapped members. And yet, if handicapped is used in the sense of a 'disadvantage or restriction of activity caused by disability'[1], the scope of the study would still have been unmanageable. Of necessity it would have to be concerned with the physically handicapped, the mentally ill, the mentally handicapped, the alcoholic and the drug addict, to name a few. Two groups of families were chosen for specific attention, those caring for the frail elderly and those caring for the severely mentally handicapped child.

Furthermore, it was believed that an analysis of these two groups of families might provide insight into the more general issue of family—State relationships and inferences might be made to those families providing care to other groups with handicapping conditions. The elderly and the mentally handicapped have been recognized as high priority groups, and the State has officially made a commitment to provide them with needed services. Their status as recipients of social services was clearly expressed as far back as the Tudor period, and since then in various Poor Law developments. In the modern phase of the Welfare State the elderly have been given high priority since 1946 and the mentally handicapped since 1959. If there are shifts occurring, if the State is in practice taking on more and more of the caring function, these shifts are likely to be found with these families.

In addressing the study questions, three sets of data were analysed: governmental statistics on expenditure and utilization of services; research studies on the elderly and the mentally handicapped; and observations from extended field visits including discussion with informed practitioners and administrators. These data were then related to a series of concepts and criteria thought to be relevant to the issue of shared responsibility between the family and the State. The purpose of this chapter then, is to reexamine the questions in light of the evidence.

Shared responsibility

Admittedly, this issue is raised in such a way that both the family and the State are assumed to have some responsibility for the provision of care to the handicapped. The legitimacy of this general proposition is rarely contested. Serious problems and disagreements emerge, however, when attempts are made to translate the concept of shared responsibility into specific social policies and programmes, for it then becomes necessary to define what functions are appropriate to each. Does the family have more responsibility than society? What does sharing mean in real terms and what is to be shared? What do families want the State to provide, and conversely, how does the State view the family? While these questions may appear to be rather philosophical and too far removed from the day-to-day operations of government, the answers to them may in fact provide insight into how policies have evolved, the shape they have taken, and most important, what kinds of policies might emerge in the future.

An analysis of family—State relationships can be guided by a set of concepts useful in characterizing the nature that the interaction has taken. Throughout this book themes have been introduced that attempt to identify the purpose of various policies. Policies have been described as those that primarily substitute for the family and those that attempt to support the family. While these terms suggest a dichotomy, that each is exclusive of the other, dichotomies have limited value and often do not reflect reality. A more reasonable way of exploring the issue is to postulate that there is a range of policies, and specific policies may have multiple purposes. Policies might then be located on a continuum whose end points are extreme forms of substitution and support. The needs of individuals and families vary in time and over time, and ideally the State responds to those variations with policies that support the family when it needs support and substitute for it when it does not exist or is incapable of meeting its members' needs. Even this postulation is incomplete since it suggests a progression from no services to support services to substitute services, the last only when the family breaks down. In many cases, a family may need 'substitute services' before this point is reached and before serious problems occur. Examples that come to mind are child abuse, serious neglect of the elderly, and marital disintegration. Some families may actually find themselves providing care to the handicapped long after this is desirable, and where it may be harmful to the person cared for as well as for the other family members. From this perspective both functions are necessary and neither should be viewed as more important than the other.

However, if policies and programmes are categorized by purpose or function, the State has placed greater emphasis on those that in essence substitute for the family, an emphasis that is expressed in both the scale of social welfare expenditure and the type of services developed. The reasons why this has occurred are complex and while the rationale may have changed over time, the net effect has been the same. Social services that attempt to support the family have received lower priority than those that replace the family.

So strong a statement needs some clarification. It is quite clear that if a financial yardstick is used, a far greater transfer is made to the elderly through retirement pensions, supplementary benefits, rent rebates and tax allowances than through the personal social services. While 3 per cent of the elderly may be living in institutions and up to 10 per cent may receive one or more domiciliary care services, virtually all benefit from the income transfer programmes. Furthermore, it is because of these benefits that most of the elderly are able to remain in the community. In the terms of this study, these services still substitute for those functions undertaken by families in the past. In essence, the State has assumed the responsibility of providing for the financial needs of the elderly, a responsibility that children had under the Poor Law. Beginning with the 1911 Pension Act, the elderly were no longer to be a 'burden' on their children. Instead they would be provided with income and retain some independence. The pension was not given to the children caring for their aged parents (in this sense it would be supportive to the family) but to the pensioner, and thus the State took over from or substituted for the family.

The personal social services allow for the possibility of supporting the family as well as the individual; yet institutional care services are allocated over half of the personal social service budget and provide services to a relatively small number of people. Community care services, a potential source of support to families caring for the handicapped, are channelled primarily to those without families.

This relative emphasis goes back to the early days of the Poor Law. As far back as the seventeenth century and as recently as this century the State explicitly operated on the assumption that the family had the legal and moral responsibility to meet the needs of its members. While the Poor Law approach affirmed State responsibility, this began only when the family had experienced problems in social functioning. Public services or assistance would be made available usually as a last resort and families had to admit to a form of 'family bankruptcy' or family failure. The State would then become totally responsible for the care of the individuals. While specific policies changed over the centuries and the emphasis shifted from outdoor relief to care in workhouses, the intent of the policy remained the same. If families found it necessary to seek help there was something wrong with them and their failure was a symptom of some moral inadequacy. If they were to receive assistance, they were required to place themselves under the care of the State. The evolution to policies favouring institutional care became dominant in the nineteenth century and to some extent was the logical extension of the State's view of how it should intervene. Families who were experiencing difficulty and needed support, could hardly view the State positively. If they found it necessary to seek assistance, they knew the process would involve stigmatization and in many instances the social services were provided in a punitive manner. Given this, it can be speculated that most families sought help reluctantly and only after their difficulties became somewhat unbearable.

This residual response on the part of the State has been widely criticized throughout this century. It has been described as degrading to those who sought help, counterproductive to the real goal of achieving social welfare, and firmly entrenched in questionable first principles. Still, the Poor Law offered a complete and relatively coherent system, totally consistent with prevailing moral and philosophical beliefs[2]. There was little ambiguity under this system and recipients or consumers of the social services were quite clear as to what the State would provide and what costs were involved. The twentieth century saw a marked shift in attitudes, a more enlightened conception of what poverty and other forms of social dependency entailed. The reactive function of the State was widely viewed as inadequate and pressures began to mount for more positive social measures.

The most notable of these early departures were the development of various income maintenance programmes for the elderly and the un-employed leading some to point to the 1911 social legislation as the birth of the modern Welfare State. However, this shift and subsequent legisla-tion did not represent a complete break from the past. Rather, it might be better understood as an evolutionary process that retained some elements from the past and interwove these with new ways of looking at the needs of people. The two world wars had a significant impact in that they exposed the reality that human need and misery were not only found among the poor but across social classes and demonstrated the inade-quacies of the existing market (including social mechanisms such as insurance and voluntary organizations). The net result of this evolutionary process is the existence of a wide range of social policies and programmes that are no longer internally consistent. The modern social welfare system may be more enlightened than that of the Poor Law era, but it has also produced a number of ambiguities. Today the State may verbalize a policy of social support to balance the more historical policy of social substitu-tion, but because of perceived economic limitations, it has had to establish hierarchies of social priority. The debasing means test of the Poor Law era has been replaced with the more human needs test as a rationing device, but it might be argued that the essence of practice has not changed.

For example, the recent emphasis on community care is offered as a major departure. The principle was introduced in the National Health Service Act, 1946, and the National Assistance Act, 1948, and has been reaffirmed in various Acts and White Papers since then. Community care, however, is an ambiguous concept itself and covers multiple purposes. One overriding concern of the postwar Welfare State was Poor Law reform (or, as some have suggested, its destruction). A primary target was the existing network of large institutions — the workhouses and the mental hospitals. The major intent of this particular reform, however, must be kept clear. It was not to deemphasize the provision of care in institutions but to humanize institutional care. Community care, in large part, has come to mean institutional care in the community, and not family care. The State would still function as a substitute family but would do so in a more attractive environment. As articulated in the Commons debate on National Assistance in 1947:

Therefore, we have decided to make a great departure in the treatment of old people. The workhouse is to go. Although many people have tried to humanize it, it was in many respects an evil institution. We have deter-mined that the right way to approach this problem is to give welfare authorities, as we shall now describe them, the power to establish special homes[3].

The position is found underlying policies affecting the mentally handi-capped. Throughout the 1950s the pressure was to do away with the large hospitals and to relocate the mentally handicapped in community-based residential care facilities. The 1971 White Paper placed considerable priority on this objective. The gross numbers of mentally handicapped in institutional settings would not be effected but the type and form of the institution would be quite different[4].

The elderly and the mentally handicapped would be provided care in small, home-like settings close to their families, thus creating an environment more normal and familiar. It was further hoped that by effecting this change in location, the residents would have ongoing contact with their families and friends. In essence, however, this meant that when an elderly or mentally handicapped person was residing in an institutional setting in most cases the family had a secondary role to the State, which continued to provide the major caring function. The family when it maintained contact with its relative supported the State's function.

Gradually these institutions took on another function. While many of the residents once admitted were there for long periods, the value of short-term relief for families began to emerge. It was felt that if a number of places in homes for the elderly were set aside, children or other relatives caring for their parents could be relieved periodically. The data in Chapter 4 clearly shows how the 'institutions' for the mentally handicapped have been used in this way. This practice, without question, is a significant effort to offer supportive services to families. The State may substitute for the family on a temporary basis but the purpose of the service is not to replace the family. The critical thing that needs to be emphasized here is that institutional care can have multiple purposes and services that substitute for the family can be permanent or temporary. The more important issue is one of effecting some balance in the way the resources are allocated.

A second major component of this shift to community care (or more appropriately, care in the community) was the development of those services whose primary objective was to enable the elderly and the mentally handicapped (for that matter all handicapped) to continue living in non-institutional settings. It was believed that such provision could prevent or delay a need for institutional care. If the handicapped person could not manage on his own, and if appropriate help was not readily available from family members, relatives or friends, a range of supportive services would be provided. These included the provision of more suitable housing, or physical adaptations to the home, meals, help with housekeeping, shopping and personal care, advice, counselling and social support.

While this policy of community care is viewed as one of providing support for the handicapped person, in the reference terms of this study it is more appropriately classified as care substituting for the family. The evidence cited in previous chapters shows that by far the greatest majority of the elderly handicapped are either living with their family, or receiving support from their family even when they are not living with them. Recipients of the personal social services (unlike the income maintenance and health services which are universal) are likely to be living alone, or married couples with less than adequate family resources available to them. These services are clearly supportive to the handicapped person and are instrumental in allowing him to remain in the community. However, their basic purpose is to substitute for the family. Their primary focus is the individual or couple without a family network to fall back on and, as such, are not deployed as family support services.

If the practice is to channel community resources to those dependent and handicapped, as in most cases, there are exceptions. The thrust of this argument is that higher priority is given to those not living with their family, with the rationale that they are of higher risk and have greater need. Of course, families receive and benefit from community social services. Families with mentally handicapped children have been supported through the provision of day care services, special schools and training centres. Children providing care for their elderly parents have received domiciliary services. The issue is one of degree. If proportionately more of the services go to those handicapped without families, the emphasis can be seen as one where the substitutive function outweighs the supportive function. It is not the specific service that distinguishes or differentiates between substitution and support but the reason for its provision. The service itself can be used to carry out either function.

And yet, the messages of the Seebohm Report and the 1970 statement of the Secretary for Social Services were unequivocal. In their view 'the primary purpose of the Personal Social Services was to strengthen the capacity of the family to care for its members and to supply the family's place where necessary'. Both functions, support and substitution, carry at least equal weight and substitution is not given a higher priority. However, it is becoming more and more clear that less attention and lower priority, for example, in the allocation of resources, have been given to the notion of support.

In examining the needs of the elderly and their families, it was pointed out (Chapter 3) that research beginning with Townsend's efforts in the 1950s, complemented with studies undertaken by Harris and Hunt in the late 1960s, suggest that the bulk of social care needed by the elderly is provided not by the State but through a family support network. Furthermore, local authorities appear to allocate their services primarily to the elderly without families. Finally, if patterns of social welfare expenditure are analysed, disproportionately more resources are given to institutional care services. The situation is not too different among other groups of handicapped. For example, in 1972–73 total revenue expenditure on personal social services (England and Wales) amounted to £390.5 million[5]: 42 per cent of the total was used for services to the elderly and 68 per cent of this for residential care. Services for the mentally handicapped accounted for 6 per cent of the total, services for the younger physically handicapped 3 per cent, and for the mentally ill less than 1 per cent. Across all client categories, one-half or £166.5 million of all personal services went to residential care.

In the previous chapter a number of factors were identified to provide some explanation for this imbalance. Lack of resources was proposed as a major barrier. When resources are perceived to be scarce, a hierarchy of needs is often introduced. Yet, by definition, resources are never adequate. Resources have grown substantially over several decades both in absolute and in relative terms. The way that resources are organized and deployed as well as the attitudes and practice patterns of the providers of the services were seen as two additional barriers. There is another issue that is of a different dimension. It is possible that it is easier to plan for services that substitute for the family assuming that resources, both capital and staff, are available. These services lend themselves to a structured approach while family support services create all sorts of programming difficulties.

For example, in planning for social services over the past fifteen years heavy reliance has been placed on various national surveys. These studies, many of which have been cited in this book, have taken as the unit of analysis the handicapped individual. The data report on the characteristics of the handicapped: their capacities and incapacities, the degree of the handicap, their socio-economic status and their living status. For planning purposes the handicapped are then grouped by age, sex, and the severity of their condition. These data lend themselves to aggregations and a set of programmes can be developed for the sub-groups. Furthermore, handicap is usually defined in terms of the ability to carry out basic functions. How many of the handicapped are mobile, how many can bathe, feed and care for themselves? How many live alone? Given these aggregate data on the handicapped, the planner can begin to translate them into specific service plans. Needs, a vague but crucial conceptual starting point, are thus linked to an identification of tasks or functions necessary for social and physical wellbeing.

If the handicapped person does not have a family, or in the case of many elderly, the handicapped person lives with a spouse, the planning process is relatively straightforward. If the person is severely handicapped and needs total care, the outcome is likely to be residential care where the social service staff assumes those functions normally carried out by a family. The handicapped person is provided with a room, meals, health and personal care services, and social stimulation in a total caring environment. The residential care facility becomes the home and the staff and other residents function as a substitute family. The planning task becomes one of estimating the number of handicapped who fall into this category and then designing the necessary services.

Where the handicapped person can manage reasonably if certain functions are taken over, the task becomes one of assessing the individual's incapacity and then providing what is necessary. Again, the available surveys are useful. Once norms or standards are established and functions delineated, needs can be aggregated and services designed systematically.

It is much more difficult to plan for those situations where the handicapped person is living with his family, where the family has assumed the major caring responsibility. First of all, the focus has shifted from the handicapped person, a shift that is more significant than may appear on the surface. The task is no longer one of assessing an individual's capacity to function and then providing services that either totally or partially substitute for the family. What is required now is the provision of services that ease the management task of the family. If planning requires an ability to categorize need and then a capability for aggregation, the process logically begins with a search for similarities between individuals rather than a focus on their differences. For example, what do families caring for the handicapped have in common? This search for common need is difficult when families are providing care in so far as their support needs vary widely. It has been suggested furthermore that an important criteria of a caring society is flexibility, but flexibility is often viewed by planners to be antithetical to the need to structure services. In Marshall's opinion, this is the fundamental dilemma faced by Titmuss: 'Only through discretionary welfare is it possible to disperse what he [Titmuss] called flexible individualized justice and, more fundamentally, that there is no such thing as collective welfare, but only collective measures to promote individual welfare'[6].

Is it possible then, to plan collective measures, requiring that need be standardized and aggregated, to meet the needs of individual families effectively? If this is a factor in why family support services have not been more fully developed or might not be even when the economic situation is reversed, it should be looked at more closely. It might be necessary to begin to search for similarities of need among families, even if the idea of similarity has to be stretched. This line of argument would suggest that surveys (even of a small scale) and other types of research should be initiated, but studies where the unit of analysis becomes the family of the handicapped and not the handicapped person. The studies of families cited in preceding chapters are beginning points, but they need to be expanded. There is much to be learned by systematically asking families themselves what types of support they would find helpful. These data might then provide the categorical and aggregate data required for the planning process.

There is enough evidence available from interviews with families to identify the need to include relief from the pressure of providing full-time care, support in overcoming a sense of social isolation, financial assistance, housing and practical help. Families also express a need to feel that someone is interested in and cares for them. Even without the benefit of additional research, some steps might be taken. If existing policies encourage a number of places in residential care facilities be set aside to provide short-term relief for families, to achieve this policy objective they must be protected even if there is a waiting list of people requiring long-term care. Additionally, local authorities might reassess their existing residential care population. One such governmental survey showed that 45 per cent of all permanent elderly residents in England were minimally dependent; 38 per cent moderately dependent and 17 per cent substantially dependent. Minimally dependent included all those residents who were continent, mobile without assistance, able to feed themselves and alert[7]. Conceivably, some proportion of this group, which represents almost one of every two residents, could manage adequately in less institutionalized settings if appropriate community services were provided. While these services would still represent a substitutive function, some of the residential care places might be freed for short-term relief of the family. Such an approach is a fair example of the multiple purposes of specific services.

This section began by introducing the idea of shared responsibility and reasonable boundaries to the State's intervention. The issue is relevant because many fear that the State may have overstepped its appropriate role, inadvertently weakened the family as a social institution and actually encouraged families to transfer the caring function to the State. The concept of sharing implies services to support families and yet, in the context of this study, the State has emphasized a substitutive function. Since there are fewer resources allocated to support families it could be concluded that there is relatively little sharing and a movement towards reasonable boundaries would result in the State doing much more. A potential danger of the present approach is that in giving lower priority to family support services families may be forced to relinquish the caring function. As the care and management of the handicapped person becomes more difficult, the social, physical and financial costs may become impossible. Does the evidence show that this is occurring?

Family responsibility in a Welfare State

The idea that the presentday family is less willing to function as the primary, first-line caring institution has gained considerable currency. To some degree, it is accepted as a fact by many people. For others it is a valid hypothesis that only requires to be demonstrated. In the course of this enquiry this issue was posed to scores of civil servants and social welfare practitioners throughout England and Wales as well as in Denmark and the Federal Republic of Germany. A number of additional contacts were made with key representatives from the voluntary health and welfare sector. They were asked two basic questions. In their opinion was this trend occurring and if so, what could they identify as factors influencing the shift?

Their comments are revealing. With a few exceptions, there appeared to be general agreement that families *are* less willing to provide their members with the level of social care that families of previous generations had given. Few were able, when pressed, to offer evidence. Rather, civil servants, planners and administrators pointed to increased demand for the social services and the State's need to find more and more social welfare resources to meet this demand. Front-line practitioners, on their part, who had direct contact with families (for example, physicians, nurses, social workers, and residential care staff) based their conclusions on impressions of current caseloads. Their impressions have to be tempered by the fact that most of the community social service personnel were relatively young and had little in the way of an historical perspective (they were not working ten to fifteen years ago) and the staff in institutions (geriatric and rehabilitation units, homes for the elderly, and mental hospitals) were likewise limited by the fact that they only come into contact with families seeking institutional care for their aged parents or mentally handicapped children. Both groups, the community and institutional practitioners, commented with little actual data and from a rather narrowly defined frame of reference.

When asked to speculate on why this was occurring, their response fell into three broad categories. The first type of 'cause' was related to the idea that in its evolution and expansion, the Welfare State itself has adversely affected the family's willingness to provide social care. Whether intended or not, a growing Welfare State has weakened the family. In providing greater amounts of social welfare resources, expectations have been raised and new demand stimulated. The interesting thing here is that this rationale was posed in all three countries, yet each country differs significantly in its form of Welfare State and the extent to which the State intervenes and the form the intervention has taken.

A second theme identified the reason in the changing nature of the family. The family in their view has changed, and is less capable of functioning as a major social institution. This position is similar to the thesis outlined in Chapter 2. The nuclear family is the dominant family type and as such cannot function in the same way as the extended family of the nineteenth and eighteenth centuries. Those who offered this rationale then argued that the expanding Welfare State is a necessary societal response. Whereas the first argument suggests that the Welfare State weakened the family, this line of reasoning begins with the idea of an already weakened family to which the State responds.

The third group sees the issue in entirely different dimensions. The smallest group of interviewees agreed that families are less willing or capable, but pointed to the nature of the State's intervention and the way in which it attempts to meet social need as the reason. In giving higher priority (that is in raising the level of social welfare expenditure beyond the universal income maintenance programmes) to services that substitute for the family it has placed too little emphasis (again in relation to the volume of expenditure) on those services intended to support families. The outcome is that families find themselves in a difficult position and over the long run the State will be forced to take over the caring function.

The surprising thing in all these discussions was that no one suggested that the scale of social dependency has been shifting over the decades and that increased demand for service is merely reflecting this shift. There are more elderly in absolute numbers than ever before. Not only that, but the elderly themselves are living longer and thus are likely to be handicapped. Fifty or even twenty-five years ago there might have been less demand simply because fewer were surviving into old age. The issue of intergenerational support was seen as less critical because there were fewer three-generational families. The same operates with regard to the severely mentally handicapped. If this is the case, it becomes more difficult to defend the position that families are less willing to provide care even if there is greater utilization.

Even with these caveats, what has the historical experience been? Based on trends in utilization data and available research, there is no clear evidence that the State is assuming the primary responsibility for the handicapped or that families want it to do so. Still, it must be underlined that in limiting the analysis to these data sources, it cannot be concluded that families are providing this care willingly or that if additional resources were made available they would not transfer more responsibility to the State. It can be concluded, however, that there is no factual basis to support the charge that the Welfare State has encouraged a discernible shift in traditional family patterns of care.

The analysis first examined patterns of institutional care. This form of social care can be viewed as the transfer of complete responsibility to the State, whether it be permanent or temporary. It was proposed that institutional care, representing a transfer of complete responsibility, might be used as a surrogate of broader trends. In practice, once admitted to institutions the elderly tend to stay there for long periods of time, often until they die. And yet current rates of institutionalization are significantly lower than those of the early years of this century — a pre-Welfare State era. Even in the 1950s when the rates were considerably lower, much of the difference can be directly attributed to the changing age structure. Since 1951 the number of elderly over the age of eighty-four has increased by 117 per cent and it is from this group that the greatest number of admissions come. The institutional rates for men aged sixty-five to eighty has actually dropped since 1958 and has remained constant for women in this age group. Those who are being admitted currently are likely to be frail, unable to manage for themselves, and have no one available to provide care. Trends in institutional care for the mentally handicapped are more complex. While the rate of institutionalization has not changed over the past twenty years (1.32 per 1,000 population), the institution itself has taken on a different function. In the 1940s and 1950s, once the mentally handicapped person was admitted, he was likely to stay in the institution. Of those admitted in 1949, 81 per cent were still institutionalized after two years, 68 per cent after six years. Of those admitted in 1959, the percentages were 51 and 40 per cent respectively. By the mid-1960s there were seventy discharges for every hundred admissions. The overall institutional rate had not changed but the rate of admissions had trebled and short-term stays were common practice. Based on institutional census figures, 70 per cent of severely handicapped children and one-half of all severely mentally handicapped of all ages are living with their families.

The point was made that these institutional trends are inconclusive. They represent the relationship between existing institutional places and effective demand on them. If the number of places were to be limited in the future, rates of institutionalization would decrease. It would be erroneous to conclude that this would show a greater willingness on the part of the family to carry the major caring function. Furthermore, if additional institutional resources were to be developed without a corresponding increase in community services the likelihood is that they would be used. It would be just as fallacious to point to these increased rates as evidence of less willingness on the part of families. For example, the State has proposed a provision rate of twenty-five residential care places per 1,000 elderly (an increase of 20 per cent from current levels) and the provision of 1.58 institutional places (mentally handicapped) per 1,000 population (an increase of 14 per cent). Could it be concluded that if rates of institutionalization exceeded these levels families were transferring more of the caring function, were less willing to carry responsibility? Probably not, since they are basically estimates of what might be necessary. For example, the rate of institutionalization for the mentally handicapped in Denmark was 1.89 per 1,000 population in 1973, a rate 20 per cent higher than the Department of Health and Social Security proposed target. Their rates of residential care for the elderly are almost twice as high as those of the United Kingdom[8]. Are their rates excessive or are the rates in this country too low? To answer this a large number of factors would have to be examined. Are the aged in both countries similar or do they exhibit marked differences? Do the elderly in either country prefer not to live with their families? For example, it may be significant that the wealthy in Great Britain developed the 'dower house' for the widowed aged parent — a home near but not with the children. The dower house could be viewed as an alternative social system just as community social services are alternatives to institutional care. If inferences were to be made about the differences in institutional trends between the countries, the analysis would have to go beyond these trends and include an assessment of the total array of social services available in each country.

When utilization trends of the community-based services are examined the conclusion is the same — there is no strong evidence to support the position that families are giving up the caring function.

Although expenditure on social welfare programmes has increased significantly over the past decade, practice has been and, given recent government policy, will continue to be the provision of social services to those handicapped who are not living with or near their families. Even if resources were doubled and utilization trebled, this growth in the community care services could be absorbed by the handicapped who are living alone or without a viable family network. For example, over the past fifteen years, almost one of every four elderly and one of every five handicapped elderly live alone. Additionally, 40 per cent of the elderly live just with their spouse, 32 per cent of the handicapped elderly. And yet, even after tremendous expansion in the domiciliary services, only 7 per cent of the elderly were receiving home help services, or health visiting services, between 9 and 10 per cent home nursing, and slightly less than 3 per cent weekly meals on wheels[9]. Even if utilization were to continue growing at the same rate, or at a faster rate, it is unlikely that the needs of those elderly without families could be met. The data on the use of the domiciliary services by families with mentally handicapped children, while sketchy, suggests the same pattern. While day care and training centre places have expanded, there is a considerable shortfall in the estimated number of places needed.

This analysis of utilization data suggests that families are implicitly expected to provide care for their handicapped parents and children. Beyond the income maintenance programmes (this will be discussed in the next section) they are receiving relatively little in the way of services that might support them to carry out this function. Those services that could support them are underdeveloped in terms of the numbers of families with handicapped members and tend to be provided to those handicapped without families. Families have expressed their frustration and feel that they are being neglected. However, they still continue to provide social care.

The issue of family policy

A third general question raised in Chapter 1 is closely related to the issue of family policy. As new social policies are enacted and translated into specific programmes, or as existing policies are modified, are they based on a realistic understanding of the present day family, its ability and attitude towards providing care to the socially dependent, or do they assume a concept of the family that is perhaps outmoded or one that never existed? It was suggested that most social policies have been developed with a major emphasis on individuals and benefits and services have been planned to meet individual need. There are some notable exceptions to this (such as the prewar family means test) but by and large they were negative family policies. There are policies that affect the elderly, the handicapped, children, the unemployed and wage earners with low income. If pressed on the issue of family policy, those responsible for the development of the legislation or its implementation will often respond that in providing a service to an individual family member the entire family will benefit; and yet this assumption should be offered as a hypothesis to be tested rather than as fact. In those instances where the explicit object of the policy is the family, the emphasis is likely to be on particular types of families, for example, single parent families, families with more than one child (family allowances), low income families (rent rebates, supplementary benefits and free school lunches), or those designated as 'multi-problem families'. The pattern appears to be one of identifying families at risk. Furthermore, social policies are built on an implicit definition of the family or at least some set of assumptions of what it is. Often, however, individual policies are at cross purposes to other policies. Many emphasize the nuclear family to the exclusion of other family types, while others recognize the existence of an extended family network.

The present situation offers a number of ambiguities. This country, like most Western countries, does not have a clearly stated policy position on the family as a social institution. Family policy in this context is defined as a 'consensus on a core of family goals' and the deliberate shaping of social policies and programmes to achieve these goals[10]. Recently, Rodgers has suggested that a family policy would also require codification[11]. A final aspect of such a policy would imply that given governmental structure, the responsibility for achieving these goals does not come under the mandate of one single agency, nor can it be constrained by departmental boundaries.

The purpose of this exploration is not to argue the value or necessity of a national policy on the family. While such a discussion could prove useful for future policy development, considerable groundwork would have to be undertaken. Moreover, a premature enactment of such a policy could result in negative effects on the family itself. For example, codification might prove to be a hindrance to new ideas, fresh adaptations and a flexible approach to meeting to the social needs of the family. This in no way argues that the idea should be ignored. There is still a need to identify and catalogue existing policies as they relate to the family. Do policies complement each other or are they contradictory and even counter-productive?

To begin with, a department by department analysis would offer some valuable insight into how each Ministry views the family, the ways that their policies affect the family, and perhaps even identify inconsistencies or contradictions between policies. This approach, however, might result in a distorted picture in so far as it ignores the interdependence of various policies. In the reference terms of this study, it is becoming clear that the health, personal social service, housing, employment, education and financial needs of families providing care for their handicapped children and parents are so closely interlocked that only a comprehensive, interdepartmental approach makes sense.

Up to this point, the major emphasis has been on those policies and programmes involving the personal social services. There were a number of reasons for so doing. First, as discussed in the previous chapter, the Seebohm Committee Report, the basis for the reorganized social services, proposed as a major objective the development of an effective family service. This was reiterated by the Secretary of State for Social Services when the proposed reorganization legislation was being debated. The idea of services to strengthen and support the capacity of families underpins the newly organized local authority departments. Second, the personal social services as defined include many of those resources needed by families providing care to the elderly and the mentally handicapped children: home helps, laundry service, transportation, day accommodation for the elderly and handicapped, meals on wheels, physical adaptations to the home, residential accommodation (for short-term relief) and community social work. Furthermore, these departments have been charged with coordinating interdepartmental service provision. For these reasons, they have to be viewed as the key to meeting the social care needs of families.

Nevertheless, family policy involves more than the personal social services. It has been pointed out on a number of occasions that 'demands made upon the personal services result from policies made elsewhere – in employment, housing, education and within the DHSS income maintenance and health services'[12]. For example, the DHSS policy emphasis on efforts to reduce hospital care for the mentally handicapped, defensible on both therapeutic and financial grounds, has brought with it increased pressure on the personal social services. The reduction of hospital places and discharges to the community has not been balanced with a comparable expansion of residential care places, other community support services and social work staff.

A decision on the part of Government to give low priority to sheltered housing schemes can also create tremendous pressures on the Social Service Department's residential care service. For example, in 1974, 24 per cent of all local authorities in England and Wales reported no expenditure on this service (36 per cent of metropolitan districts, 42 per cent of London boroughs, 5 per cent of the non-metropolitan counties). The amount of net expenditure per 1,000 population aged sixty-five and over ranged from a low of £7 to a high of £2,100; the overall average for England and Wales was £458[13]. Evidence has also been reported to show how housing policies unintentionally have had negative effects on local neighbourhoods to the point of destroying informal support networks and of physically separating children from their aged parents[14]. Once again, the personal social services are required to deal with the casualties of another department's policy.

These examples all relate to the counterproductivity of various departmental social policies. Other policies, while not necessarily at cross purposes to the effectiveness of the personal social services, do not appear to be supportive. A large number of these can be grouped under the heading of incomes policy; they include income tax, general income maintenance programmes and specialized programmes for the handicapped. Evidence was presented in earlier chapters documenting the serious financial strain experienced by most families caring for either a handicapped elderly parent or child.

A potential source of financial assistance should be the Inland Revenue service. If the cost of caring for a dependent handicapped family member is excessive and a financial burden to a family, it would seem to be reasonable that this be recognized in an income tax policy, yet for tax purposes all children are treated equally, handicapped or not. A family with a severely mentally handicapped child is entitled to the same allowance as a family with a 'normal' child of the same age. Children caring for an elderly parent receive the same tax allowance whether the parent is handicapped or not. Two allowances are related to the handicapped, the daughter's allowance and the housekeeper allowance, but they are so restrictive and the amount so small, that their contribution to the task of supporting families must been seen as negligible[15]. Furthermore, in terms of exemptions or deductions, the income tax system benefits only those families who are above the tax level, middle and upper income groups. The Department of Health and Social Security has estimated that nearly 330,000 disabled persons and their families are under the supplementary benefit level (the poverty level) and an additional 1 million are on the margins of poverty[16]. Based on the Harris survey of handicapped persons, it can be inferred that an estimated 42 per cent of impaired or disabled are in serious financial difficulty and that tax advantages are meaningless. However, for the remainder changes in the tax structure might make a financial and emotional difference. The latter benefit could actually have greater significance in so far as it demonstrates that the State does 'care' and recognizes the contribution of the family.

Various income maintenance programmes are a second potential resource. For example, in 1973 a little over 17 per cent of all public expenditure was allocated to the social security programme, or £5,500 million compared to slightly under 12 per cent for health and the personal social services[17]. Although these benefits are not specifically for handicapped persons and their families (most are either work or income related), they are being used by this group. For example, 98 per cent of the elderly were receiving social security benefits in 1971; six of every ten received only the national insurance pension and one of every four received the pension and supplementary benefits[18]. It is more difficult to identify the numbers of all handicapped receiving social security. Harris estimated that 34 per cent of the impaired were not receiving benefits, 30 per cent national insurance pensions, 20 per cent supplementary benefits and 18 per cent other benefits[19]. Four years later it was estimated that the numbers of the disabled receiving supplementary benefits had increased to 25 per cent. This increase in provision is encouraging but still means that one in five of the handicapped and their families living in or near poverty are not receiving benefits.

One incomes maintenance programme requires special attention. The constant attendance allowance, begun in 1971, is the one programme that specifically focuses on families providing care for the handicapped rather than on the handicapped person. Initially the allowance was provided in those situations where a handicapped person required frequent attention all day and most of the night. From June 1973, this was expanded to include those who needed such care either day *or* night and the benefit was established at a lower rate. By the end of 1972, 85,000 people were receiving this allowance. A year later the numbers had risen to over 150,000 (107,000 at the full rate and 45,000 at the lower rate).

This programme relates directly to the needs of families providing care to the handicapped. In fact, it is the major incomes programme that recognizes the contribution that families are making and the quickness of public response reflected in the numbers demonstrates that it was needed. However, this uptake has to be somewhat tempered when the potential target is taken into account.

Table 6.1 *Constant attendance allowances (CAA): utilization rate and prevalence of handicapping conditions, 1973, England and Wales (per 100,000 pop.)*

Age	Very severely handi- capped	Severely handi- capped	CAA higher benefit	CAA lower benefit	CAA total benefit
5–15	—	—	232	77	309
16–29	43	37	68	48	116
30–49	96	231	58	33	91
50–64	280	979	150	77	227
65–74	790	2,206	360	130	490
Over 74	3,210	4,923	1,400	450	1,850

Notes: (1) An attendance allowance is paid in respect to any person over the age of two who is so severely disabled physically or mentally that he requires frequent or continual supervision and care. Eligibility criteria are defined in the source cited below.

(2) As of 22 July 1974, those eligible for the higher rate received £8.00 per week while those eligible for the lower rate received £5.35.

(3) Very severely and severely handicapped are those categories defined by A. Harris, *Handicapped and Impaired in Great Britain*, OPCS, Social Survey Division, HMSO, 1971, pp. 13–16.

(4) Prevalence rates for those under sixteen are not available. Harris in her survey limited the study to those over fifteen years of age.

Source: DHSS, *Social Security Statistics, 1973*, GSS, HMSO, 1975, pp. 72–3.

The figures in the columns of Table 6.1 headed 'very severely handicapped' and 'severely handicapped' are estimates based on the survey carried out by Harris. Referring back to the definitions used to classify the handicapped it would appear that the very severely handicapped should be eligible for the allowance at the higher rate, while those designated as severely handicapped would be eligible for the same, or at least the lower rate. The very severely handicapped were defined as those who were:

- mentally impaired or senile, unable to understand questions or give rational answers;
- permanently bedfast;
- confined to a chair, unable to get in and out without the aid of a person;
- unable to feed themselves or need someone to assist in using the WC;
- doubly incontinent or could not be left alone since they might harm themselves.

The severely handicapped included those who:

- experienced difficulty doing everything or found most things difficult and some impossible;

- found most things difficult, or three or four items difficult and some impossible.

The pattern of utilization is somewhat difficult to interpret. While age is highly correlated with the prevalence of handicapping conditions, there is an inverse relation between age and receipt of the benefit. With the exception of those in the age group sixteen to twenty-nine (where there are more beneficiaries than the estimated number of very severely and severely handicapped) it would appear that between 20 and 25 per cent of the handicapped are receiving the attendance allowance. Even if the analysis were restricted to the very severely handicapped and assumed that those less severely handicapped were not receiving benefits, only 60 per cent of this group were likely to be covered. It has been estimated that 59,000 very severely handicapped elderly and 79,000 of the severely handicapped elderly are living with their children, yet only 72,000 received a constant attendance allowance in 1973 (54,000 at the higher rate and 18,000 at the lower rate). It can further be hypothesized that many of the recipients were not among the 138,000 handicapped living with their children. Why has the uptake been so low? Are families not applying? Are they being rejected?

These are only a few examples of various policy issues that need to be examined if a family policy is to become feasible. It involves both intra- and interdepartmental attention at both levels of Government. Until recently, such an interdepartmental approach would have proved organizationally impossible since there were no mechanisms to encourage corporate policy making and planning. However, it has been reported that the present government has created an interdepartmental structure, the Joint Approach to Social Policy (JASP), involving the Treasury, the Home Office, the Departments of Health and Social Security, Education and Science, and the Environment[20]. While this approach has been introduced primarily to deal with the economic crisis and might be viewed as a mechanism to decide where cutbacks in public expenditure might be made (a somewhat negative objective), the experience could conceivably initiate a process that will have a range of positive outcomes. Three broad objectives have been proposed: to work out priorities between departments; to improve coordination between departmental services as they affect individuals (families are not mentioned); and to recognize that social problems cut across departmental lines. Under the heading of long-term studies, the Report of the Central Policy Review Staff specifically mentions the family and suggests the need to anticipate the consequences of the 'possibly declining capacity and willingness of the family and the local community to care for their own social casualties'[21]. Although this focus on the family implies that families are in fact less willing or capable, it is encouraging that 'the family' has been recognized officially and, as such, may be the focus of an interdepartmental enquiry. This in turn might lead to a discussion on family goals and, if desirable, to a rational shaping of policies and programmes and a commitment to the financia!

and administrative support necessary to achieve these goals. If this were to occur the framework would be provided to deal with the needs of families caring for the handicapped.

Summary and conclusions

This study began with the thesis that the Welfare State as it has evolved is dependent upon (a set of basic assumptions concerning the responsibility which families assume or are expected to assume for their own members and the conditions under which this responsibility is to be shared or taken over by society through its public and voluntary organizations.) While these assumptions are inherent, this evolution has carried with it a number of ambiguities, and (the borderline between societal and family responsibility is less clear than in generations predating the modern Welfare State.) Furthermore, these ambiguities have resulted in various policy, programmatic and practice ambivalences. Given the current economic and socio-political climate, a number of key questions arise. Are certain functions more appropriate to one rather than both of these basic social institutions? (Should specific functions be retained by the family and others be transferred to the State? Is it possible to identify still other functions that might be shared by both and if so what proportion and at what time?)

While these questions may appear to be philosophical, they are real and have a direct bearing on the specific policy and programmatic actions the State is likely to propose for the near future. Although the concepts are presented in the abstract, as issues they have been appearing with mounting frequency in the political arena of many Western countries. They have not been raised as issues to be explored or questions to be examined: rather they are expressed, usually in emotive phrases, as political or ideological facts (One dominant proposition is that the Welfare State, in its expansion, has adversely affected the family's willingness or capability to provide social care and the corollary that if the expansion were to continue on its present course, the family as a social institution would become an anachronism) Their recommendations usually involve retrenchment in the scale of social welfare expenditure and withdrawal by the State from various areas.

The purpose of this book was not to debate the merits or weaknesses of this position. It has been concerned with identifying and synthesizing relevant evidence. If this shift were actually occurring, then, but only then, could the question of causation be raised. The issue of family—State responsibility is extremely complex and multi-faceted, and little systematic research has been undertaken in this area. From the beginning the decision was reached to base the enquiry on existing information sources: expenditure data, utilization trends and specific research efforts relevant to the issue. To complement these data interviews were held with various government (both central and local) and voluntary administrators, planners, and practitioners.

A number of critical concepts were introduced to guide the analysis. Services were divided into those that support the family and those that substitute for family functions. Regardless of the type of service, if the primary focus was on the handicapped person it was classified as a substitute service; if on the other hand the service was provided to the family to ease its task in caring for the handicapped member, it was viewed as a support service. Services were also differentiated on a time scale (were they provided on a temporary or permanent basis?) and on an intensity scale (if the service substituted for the family was it a partial or complete transfer?).

Building on this framework, it was pointed out that although social welfare expenditure increased considerably over the past twenty years, increases that outstripped growth in other areas of public expenditure, most of this expansion benefited individuals in need rather than the family as a social unit requiring support. Still, it appears that families are continuing to provide care and there is no evidence that families are actually transferring the caring function to the State or that they are becoming less viable social institutions.

In so far as this study relied heavily on existing data sources, the conclusions have to be limited. Although the analysis does counter the growing belief that the Welfare State has brought about changes in the family's ability to function — a critical finding in its own right — the evidence cannot be used to answer some of the more qualitative questions. Utilization trends have been and are likely to continue to be influenced by the availability of specific social welfare services. Demand, supply and rising expectations are all important factors that affect utilization and if expenditure on services that substitute for the family were to be increased at a rate disproportionate to supportive services, future trends may show increased transfers to the State. This is a possibility and as such should be treated as a hypothesis.

If the State were to do nothing it might find itself faced with a serious problem. On the other hand, if it were consciously to curtail social expenditure on the assumption that greater transfers are likely to occur, the result could be as disastrous. Neither course can be justified. Other issues, identified but not dealt with in this study, need to be examined more closely. One such possible enquiry was discussed earlier in this chapter — the analysis of existing social policies as they relate to the family. It was suggested that such an effort, intra- and interdepartmental in scope, would demonstrate whether social policies are complementary, contradictory or counterproductive to governmental actions. Such a study would also have the benefit of firmly establishing the family as a critical object of social policy, and would provide a framework to address the needs of families caring for the handicapped and socially dependent members.

Beyond this, an attempt should be made to identify the factors that influence families to continue providing care. Families have articulated their frustrations and have stated that they feel neglected by the State.

Still, the great majority continue to carry on. There is little available data to suggest that they are clearly doing so willingly. What is known is that the handicapped member is in the community, more often than not living with family members, and not in institutions. It can be hypothesized that in a given population there will be families who are coping and will continue to manage with minimal State intervention; others who are willing to provide care but need a considerable amount of support; still others who want to look after their elderly parent or handicapped child but are really incapable even with support; and finally those who are unwilling to carry out this function. Maddox draws attention to this when he suggests:

A family does not always provide a benign environment for its members. Parents do not always want the children they bear; they are not always capable of providing the resources necessary for their development as healthy, competent individuals. Spouses do not always respect, much less like each other, and the same is true of the feelings of children for their parents. Adult children do not always, and cannot always assume responsibility for their ageing parents. Families are thus sometimes the source of problems for their members; and the resources which families can and will make available to members are limited [22].

Research should be initiated to identify the distribution of these family types and attempts made to delineate the factors associated with each pattern. Why are some families willing to provide care and actually benefit from doing so? Can these factors be built on? If other families are ambivalent or feel they have little choice, what impact does this have on the family as a unit, the individual family members, and the handicapped person? What distinguishes such a study from others is that the focus would be on the family as a caring system or network and not on the individual needing care.

To further expand the information base for policy development, additional studies might usefully build on existing research related to institutionalization. It is clear that factors associated with the decision to seek institutionalization include the degree of impairment, the crowding of available living space, the perceived danger to the individual and the family unit, the perceived availability and cost of alternative arrangements, and finally the availability of family members to provide care. This last factor is probably the most crucial and was discussed in Chapter 3. Many of the studies cited earlier focused on the elderly or handicapped after they were admitted or were placed on a waiting list for institutional care. Research is now needed to identify those factors that predispose some families to institutionalize a handicapped member. Such an exploration might provide insight into the expectations adult family members share about the management of a handicapped child or parent and under what conditions they would be willing to retain that member in the community. If this were possible, appropriate support systems might be developed to prevent institutionalization in some instances and in others, to discharge family members already institutionalized. Such a strategy presupposes that the support could be provided at the appropriate time and not made available after the stress has reached the breaking point. A potential early warning or casefinding system is the mandate given to local authorities to carry out surveys of the chronically ill and disabled. Although many authorities viewed this as a one-time effort, others initiated it as an ongoing activity. A large number of requests for service were related to physical needs (e.g. for adaptations to housing and appliances). Additional requests were for holidays or other forms of short-term relief. In discussing these with local authority staff members it seems that the operating procedure was to focus only on the specific request and not to explore the issue of need and support in a broader perspective. If a study were carried out to identify factors associated with family capacity and willingness to provide care, supplemented with an exploration of those kinds of social support families perceive to be important, this information could be useful both as a diagnostic tool by those conducting the surveys of the chronically ill and as the basis for developing appropriate intervention strategies. In terms of the institutional population, if a resident is found to have a family the information could be used to initiate discussion or reopen communication with family members. The focus in this case would be on exploring the types of support a family would require if the elderly parent or handicapped child were to return home. As discussed in the preceding chapter, the cornerstones of such an approach are flexibility, choice and a reassessment of current patterns of social service deployment. To move beyond the rhetoric of family support services entails a commitment to reevaluate priorities in expenditure and a concerted effort on the part of practitioners to question what they are doing and how they are doing it.

In summary, there is no evidence that the family as such is giving up its caring function. There has been and continues to be more inter- and intragenerational contact and support than many believe to exist, despite the fact that families are required to be mobile; that fewer caretakers are available because of higher marriage rates and working mothers; that families wanting to care for elderly parents find this difficult if not impossible because of long-standing housing policies; and finally that community social services tend to be provided to individuals who either have no family or whose family has reached a decision to discontinue the caring function. The family appears to be stronger and more viable than many anticipated. This in turn has led others to suggest that the State is exploiting the family. Exploitation is, however, a strong word. It implies that the State consciously and purposely sets out to use the family unjustly for its own profit or advantage, that the State is benefiting at the expense of the family[23]. There is no doubt that the State is benefiting. The amount of social care provided by families far exceeds that undertaken by the State. It is impossible, furthermore, to assign a monetary value to it, and it is inconceivable to speculate the cost involved if the State were to become the primary caring institution. Furthermore, the State through its social welfare system cannot take over one of the most basic social functions, the provision of emotional support. Some family functions can be substituted for — for example physical care, whether this involves the provision of meals, housekeeping, a residence, recreation and income maintenance. The State is also in the position to support the family, to relieve the burden of the caring function by substituting for certain functions. Earlier the case was made that a caring society must involve some sense of a shared responsibility. The essence of sharing is a recognition of the contribution that families are making and a serious attempt to move from a unilateral relationship to one based on exchange. The State is fortunate to have families who care. The corollary to this is that families should also be supported by a caring society.

State

References

1. A. Harris, *Handicapped and Impaired in Great Britain*, OPCS, Social Survey Division, HMSO, 1971, p. 2.

2. This is not meant to imply that the prevailing beliefs were not criticized. As far back as the 1830s, we find counter positions, e.g. the Debates on the 1834 Poor Law Report. Later individuals such as Dickens, Carlyle, Mrs Gaskell and others challenged current approaches.

3. Commons Debate on National Assistance, 24 November 1947; cited in *The Rise of the Welfare State*, ed., M. Bruce, Weidenfeld and Nicolson, 1973, p. 265.

4. For example in the DHSS White Paper, *Better Services for the Mentally Handicapped*, Cmnd 4683, HMSO, 1971, the total number in institutional settings was estimated to be 65,000. This included almost 60,000 in hospitals and 5,000 in residential care facilities. A major recommendation was to effect a shift in the location of care so that the ratio of residential care to hospital places would come close to 1 : 1 (p. 42).

5. C. McCreadie, 'Personal social services', in *Inflation and Priorities*, ed., R. Klein, London, Centre for Studies in Social Policy, 1975, p. 60.

6. T. H. Marshall, 'Richard Titmuss — an appreciation', *The British Journal of Sociology*, 24, no. 2, 1973, p. 139.

7. DHSS, Statistics and Research Division 6, *The Census of Residential Accommodation, 1970*, HMSO, 1970.

8. Communication with the Danish National Board of Social Welfare, Copenhagen, March 1975.

9. Based on 1973 data and discussed in Chapter 3; see Table 3.16.

10. A. Schorr, 'Family policy in the United States', in *Explorations in Social Policy*, New York, Basic Books, 1968, p. 143.

11. B. Rodgers, 'Family policy in France', *Journal of Social Policy*, 4, no. 2, 1975, p. 113.

12. R. Clarke, 'PSSC: the first year', *Social Work Today*, 6, no. 6, 1975, p. 161.

13. *Social Services Statistics Estimates, 1974/75*, The Chartered Institute of Public Finance and Accountancy, London, October 1975.

14. M. Young and P. Willmott, *Family and Kinship in East London*, Routledge and Kegan Paul, 1957.

15. For example, to be eligible for the daughter's service allowance (an allowance of £55 per annum in 1974/75), the elderly or infirm parent (the object of the care) must actually be maintaining the daughter (the supplier of the care). The housekeepers allowance (£100 per annum, 1974/75) requires that the elderly person be a widow or widower.

16. Reported by Brian O'Malley, Minister of State at DHSS, 20 May 1974, and cited by P. Townsend, 'Help for the disabled', *New Society*, 24 July 1975, pp. 193–4.

17. CSO, GSS, Social Trends, HMSO, 1974, Table 185, p. 199.

18. Ibid., Table 36, p. 34.

19. A. Harris, op. cit. (ref. 1), extrapolated from Table 13, p. 23.

20. For a discussion of the Joint Approach to Social Policy see the lead articles 'Sharing out the misery', *The Guardian*, 24 May 1975; and 'The making of social policy' *The Times*, 24 May 1975. *The Times Educational Supplement* offers a detailed analysis of this development in 'Ministers make pact on cash for social services', 23 May 1975.

21. Central Policy Review Staff, *A Joint Framework for Social Policies*, HMSO, 1975, p. 11.

22. G. L. Maddox, 'Families as context and resources in chronic illness', *Long Term Care*, ed., S. Sherwood, New York, Spectrum Publications, 1975, p. 317.

23. *Webster's Third New International Dictionary*, Springfield, Mass., G. & C. Merrion, 1966, p. 801.

Index

Age concern, 63
American Association on Mental
  Deficiency, 67

Bayley, M., 84
*Better Services for the Mentally
  Handicapped*, 85, 121
Bone, M., 75, 77

Chronically Sick and Disabled Persons
  Act 1969, 85, 107
Constant attendance allowance, 132—4
Cresswell, J., 45

Day care, 86—7, 100, 109, 129, 130
Daughter's allowance, 131
Denmark, 12, 125, 128

Education Act 1944, 93
Education Act 1971, 85
Elementary Education Act 1899, 66
Eugenics movement, 65, 67

Family: deterioration, 6—9, 126, 134,
  138; exploitation, 45—6, 138;
  function, 15—17; mobility, 22—3,
  policy, 27—9, 129—35; structure,
  16, 24—7
Family—State relationship: shared
  responsibility, 5, 16, 95—7, 105—6,
  117; supportive v substitutive,
  9—10, 46, 51, 58, 85—7, 93—4,
  107
Federal Republic of Germany, 12, 125

Galton, Sir Frances, 65, 66
Grad, J., 45, 71, 78

Harris, A., 40, 41, 42, 43, 54, 55,
  103—4, 132
Health visitors, 52, 53, 128
Hewitt, S., 71, 82, 83
Holt, K., 70, 71
Home helps, 52, 53, 54, 55, 56, 58, 84,
  86, 100, 128
Home nursing, 52, 53—4, 55, 56, 86,
  128
Housekeeping allowance, 131
Housing, 23, 24
  sheltered, 54, 131
Hunt, A., 56, 84

Idiots Act 1886, 65
Ingleby Report on Children and Youth,
  94, 106
Inland Revenue Service, 131

Joint Approach to Social Policy (JASP),
  134
Joint Framework for Social Policies,
  Report by the Central Policies
  Review Staff, 134

Litwak, E., 30
Local Authority and Personal Social
  Services Act 1970, 85
Lowther, C., 45

Maddox, G., 137
Marshall, T. H., 93, 124
Meals on Wheels, 52, 54, 100, 129
Mental Deficiency Act 1913, 66
Mental Health Act 1959, 66, 72, 79,
  80, 94
Moncrieff, J., 82
Morris, P., 77, 78

National Assistance Act 1948, 85, 92
National Assistance Act 1962, 85, 92
National Association for the Care of the
  Feeble-Minded, 65, 67
National Health Service Act 1946, 85,
  93, 120
National Insurance Act 1946, 93, 120

Page, C., 87
Pasker, P., 45, 55
Planning support services, difficulties,
  123—4
Poor Law Institutions, 1, 46, 119, 120
Presidents Panel on Mental Retardation,
  67

Report of the Committee on Local
  Authority and Allied Personal
  Social Services (1968), 79, 97,
  105—7, 111, 122
Report of the Poor Law Commission
  (1832), 8, 64
Report of the Royal Commission on the
  Law Relating to Mental Illness and
  Mental Deficiency, 79
Report of the Wood Committee, 66, 79

Rodgers, B., 130
Rosenheim, M., 26, 46

Sainsburg, P., 45
Sandlebridge Colony, 65
Schorr, A., 9
Seebohm, *see* Report of the Committee
    on Local Authority and Allied
    Personal Social Services
Shanas, E., 27, 42, 43
Smith, R., 55
Social need, 100, 102—4, 123—5
Social Welfare, assumptions and
    ambiguities, 4—5, 92—3, 116, 120
Sorokin, P., 7, 8
Special schools, 86
Sumner, G., 55

Sussman, M., 16, 24

Titmuss, R., 18, 101, 104, 124
Tizard, J., 67—8, 71, 78, 87
Townsend, P., 39, 54—5, 59, 103
Training centres, 81, 86, 100

Volunteers, 110—11

Wager, R., 56
Wedderburn, D., 55
Welfare State, 4, 6, 7, 126, 127, 135
Williamson, J., 45
Willmott, P., 18, 28
World Health Organization, 27, 67

Young, M., 18, 28